THE DEAD JESUS
FINDING LIFE IN HIS DEATH

NORMAN MORRIS GRAY

Foreword by
JUDY JACOBS

The Dead Jesus: Finding Life in His death

Copyright © 2026 by Norman Morris Gray

Published by:

Sonrise Publishing Company

San Marcos, TX

United States of America

All rights reserved.

No part of this publication may be reproduced, distributed, or transmitted in any form or by any means, including photocopying, recording, or other electronic or mechanical methods, including information storage and retrieval systems, without the prior written permission of the publisher, except for the use of brief quotations in a book review.

Unless otherwise indicated, all Scripture quotations are taken from the *New American Standard Bible*® (NASB), Copyright © 1960, 1971, 1977, 1995, 2020 by The Lockman Foundation. All rights reserved.

Hardback ISBN: 979-8-9949293-2-2

Paperback ISBN: 979-8-9949293-0-8

Digital ISBN: 979-8-9949293-1-5

Library of Congress Control Number: 2026907186

Cover concept—Norman Morris Gray

Cover design—Adriel Norman Gray and Leena Dass

Printed in the United States of America

DEDICATION

To the women who shaped every page of this book —

Veena Gloriana Gray -Mother
You faced storms that would have broken most, yet you never broke. Through loss, poverty, and the long silence of unanswered questions, you showed us what courage truly looks like — not the absence of fear, but the decision to walk through it, head held high, hand in hand with God. Thank you for raising three children who fear the Lord. That is your greatest legacy, and it will outlast us all.

Jyoti Anthony -Sister
When the moment demanded more than most people would give, you gave it without hesitation. Your resilience has never been loud — it has always been faithful, steady, and beautifully devoted to God and to this family. Thank you for being the kind of courage that does not announce itself—it simply shows up when it is needed most.

Supriya Gray -Wife

_You stared death in the face and chose faith. When doctors
spoke of endings, you fixed your eyes on Jesus and refused to
look away. Your faith did not waver; it carried our family
through the valley and into the light. Thank you for standing
beside me in life and in ministry, for every sacrifice made in
the shadow of the spotlight, and for being living proof that
resurrection is not just a doctrine — it is a life fully
surrendered to the One who conquered death._

Judy Jacobs -Prophetic Voice

_Some books are written. This one was spoken into existence.
Before a single word was on the page, God used your voice to
call this book forth — a prophetic declaration that would not
return void. Thank you for being a woman who hears heaven
clearly and speaks it boldly — even when the one receiving it
cannot yet see what God already has._

**_"Strength and dignity are her clothing, and she
smiles at the future."_**
PROVERBS 31 : 25

CONTENTS

ENDORSEMENTS

In his book, *The Dead Jesus*, my friend Norman Morris Gray shares, through the revelation of Scripture and personal challenge-to-victory stories, that every Biblical and historical miracle of Jesus — ultimately His resurrection — has a true and powerful eternal impact. This is an instantly life-changing book, full of fire.

-Jamie Tuttle

Lead Pastor, Dwelling Place Church International, Cleveland, TN

Pastor Norman Morris Gray writes with theological depth and pastoral honesty, inviting readers to wrestle with the cross, the cost of faith, and the life found only in Christ. This is a Christ-centered work that will strengthen believers, challenge assumptions, and point hearts to the power of the risen Jesus.

-Jon Jon Wilkins

Lead Pastor, City Life Church, San Francisco, CA

Chairman, Ministers' Fellowship International, USA

It is one of the great honors of my life and ministry to serve alongside Norman Morris Gray at PromiseLand. Having walked with him in India and witnessed firsthand the places and pain that shaped his story, I can say this book is not theory — it is testimony. Norman does not write about the resurrection as an abstract doctrine but as the sustaining power that carried him from childhood loss and poverty to courageous faith, church planting, personal tragedy, and relentless hope. His life and message are inseparable. With theological depth and disarming vulnerability, he invites us to confront a question that cannot remain intellectual: Is Jesus truly alive — and if so, what must change in us? This book will challenge, strengthen, and awaken every reader who dares to take the empty tomb seriously.

-Robin Steele

Senior Pastor, PromiseLand Church, San Marcos, TX

In *The Dead Jesus — Finding Life in His Death*, Pastor Norman Morris Gray opens the door to his own journey through loss, pain, and seasons of deep darkness. He weaves Biblical truth seamlessly through his story, inviting us to confront our own doubts and wrestle honestly with what remains when certainty falls away. With raw honesty and theological insight, Norman walks the reader through suffering, showing how the death of Jesus gives rise to a hope that is real, resilient, and rooted in the resurrection. This book has stirred my faith and renewed my hope — thank you, my friend.

-Bryan E.W. Davis

Lead Pastor, LifeSpring Church, Abbotsford, BC
Ministers' Fellowship International, Canada

In *The Dead Jesus*, Norman Morris Gray weaves his unique experience and deep understanding of Scripture into a compelling narrative that is both personal and powerfully instructive. I came away inspired to know this Jesus the way Norman does. Read it, and I believe you too will be strengthened and compelled to experience the power of His resurrection. With pastoral clarity and spiritual urgency, Norman challenges readers to move beyond passive belief into a living, transformative relationship with the risen Christ. This book is not merely informative — it is an invitation to awakening and deeper discipleship.

-Andrew Cromwell
Lead Pastor, Koinonia Church, Hanford, CA

Every page invites the Holy Spirit to challenge and transform your heart through conviction, compassion, love, and truth. Through this reading you will gain a deeper understanding of how the Living God can resurrect what feels like death in your life. Pastor Norman does a beautiful job of intertwining his lived experience and the Scripture to display the communal healing and resilience that is possible with Christ. I suggest this as an essential read through your healing journey. May the Lord use this book to deepen your understanding of His role through the highs and lows in your life.

-Dr. Deserah Telles PhD
LPC LCDC, Tell Us Counseling, Austin, TX

The Dead Jesus is powerful, intriguing, and beautifully written. From the first page, Pastor Norman Morris Gray pulls you in and doesn't let go. It's challenging, faith-stretching, and deeply engaging page to page. This is the kind of book that makes you stop, think, and then keep reading because you have to know what's next. You won't be able to put it down. You're going to love it. I highly recommend you read this.

-Beau James Norman
Lead Pastor, The Hill, Stockton, MO

Pastor Norman Morris Gray shares a deeply personal and spiritually compelling journey into the heart of Christian faith. It is an honest reflection on the transforming power of Christ's sacrifice and resurrection. Norman shares his personal journey of faith, struggles, and renewal, inviting readers to discover true life through the meaning of the cross. A moving and inspiring testimony that will resonate with anyone seeking deeper faith and understanding. It has been a blessing for me and my family to be an integral part of Norman's and his family's lives.

-Augustus Anthony
Bishop, Assembly of Believers Church in India

In his book, The Dead Jesus, Pastor Norman Gray wrestles with a very stirring question:

"Would you still be a Christian if Jesus was never raised from the dead?"

In our Christian belief, the resurrection from the dead is a primary focus of the Christian life. It is the premise from which we get our faith, our life experiences, our knowledge for raising our family, but most of all, our hope for the afterlife.

Everything I have ever done, accomplished, and built my life upon is founded on the fact that Jesus Christ is alive. He was crucified, placed in a tomb, and rose on the third day according to Scripture. (1 Corinthians 15:3-4) Pastor Norman, in this thought-provoking book, and I may add a powerful, strong, and anointed work appointed by God, is causing me to see through the lens of faith anew and afresh.

Having served the Lord for many decades, since a young child, I have seen the miracles, I have experienced the unbelievable and have had the power of God manifested in my life, so there is no question in my mind that Jesus Christ lives today. That's not because my mother and father taught me that as a child born and raised in church, but it is because of my own experiences with Jesus, that I have a living, working, and convincing evidence that He is who He says He is.

On the other hand, as Pastor Norman has so meticulously fleshed out throughout this work, there are times when life seemingly crushes you, circumstances will overwhelm you, and facts will stare you in the face that want to utterly defy the truth that Jesus is alive. But because I walk with Him every day, enjoy His peace, His presence, and His assurance that is as close to me as the very breath that I breathe, there is no question in my mind that Jesus is the Lily of the Valley, the Bright and Morning Star, the Alpha and Omega, and the Beginning and the End.

In this life stirring book, expect to find encouragement in the middle of discouragement and peace with answers in the middle of chaos.

You will draw strength from Pastor Norman's words of life experiences, that there will be absolutely no question in your mind that Jesus is the sweet, loving, and kind savior that He is. Unlike other leaders and philosophers that lived and now they are dead...many of them you can go to their tombs and find that they are in fact still dead...there is one tomb you can visit and realize that Jesus is alive and He is alive forevermore.

My family and I have had the privilege of ministering alongside of Pastor Norman and Supriya and their two precious sons in the beautiful country of India on many occasions. We find them to be solid, God honoring, and powerful lovers of Jesus. I rejoice with him as this prophetic word spoken over him is birthed and my prayer is that thousands, even millions, will come to know this Jesus who is not dead as Pastor Norman testifies to, but that Jesus is alive and very active in the lives of mankind. Be blessed as you read this book and meditate on the goodness of God. Blessings and Grace. Ephesians 3:20.

- ***Judy Jacobs***
    Internationally renowned Worshipper, Author,
    Mentor and host of PURSUIT Women's Conference
    Dwelling Place Church International
    His Song Ministries, Cleveland, TN

**_Would you still be a Christian if Jesus had never
risen from the dead?_**

I've asked this question to thousands of Christians across
five continents—in Asia, the Americas, Africa, and Europe.
In megachurches and house churches. To pastors and new
believers. To theologians and teenagers. To people I've
preached for and people I've never met before.

The answer has been consistent. Every single person
said no. Here are some of their replies:

"No, if Jesus is dead, Christianity is pointless."

"If He didn't rise, there's no hope."

"Without the resurrection, we're just following another
dead religion."

Every Christian I've spoken to agrees: without the resurrection, they wouldn't be Christian. The resurrection is the
most important event in Christianity and in the life of a
believer.

But here's my follow-up question, the one that cuts

deeper: ***Why wouldn't you be a Christian if Jesus never rose from the dead?***

Here's what I've witnessed being born and raised in India, traveling the world, and living among diverse faiths:

Hindus worship with utter devotion. Their myths speak of cycles, but no historical figure conquered death. Yet they wake before dawn for worship, fast, make pilgrimages, dedicate entire lives to gods who never left their graves.

Muslims follow Islam with radical commitment. Muhammad died in 632 AD and stayed dead. Yet they pray five times daily without fail, fast for Ramadan, and show remarkable discipline in their faith.

Sikhs follow ten Gurus with acts of service that are exemplary in many religions. They feed strangers, serve in disasters, embody selfless love—all following teachers who offered no resurrection, no victory over death. Buddhists become monks, sacrifice everything—possessions, family, comfort—for Buddha, dead 2,500 years. He offered no promise of conquering death. Just a path to enlightenment.

Let that sink in: billions follow dead prophets with radical, life-altering devotion. And here's what humbles and challenges me as a Christian: ***if they can be that devoted without the resurrection, what excuse do our comforts have?***

Even without rising, Jesus is still worthy of everything we have.

I say this not to shake your faith, but to strengthen it—to help us all examine what truly drives our devotion. Because even without resurrection, Jesus is still the most profound teacher who ever lived. His ethics are revolutionary. His love is transformative. His sacrifice is unmatched. His teachings alone could change the world.

Let me open up my heart. I am writing this as someone who loves and treasures the Church deeply. My whole life has been poured into serving God's people, and I wouldn't trade that calling for anything. But sometimes love requires honest conversation about where we've settled for less than God intended. This isn't a spotlight on others—it's a mirror I'm choosing to stand in front of first.

So why does His resurrection matter so much to us? We believe He did rise. We believe He conquered death. We believe He's alive right now.

So the *real question* becomes even more pressing.

WHAT I WITNESSED GROWING UP IN INDIA

I grew up in Lucknow, India, where every morning sounded like a symphony of prayers. The Muslim call to prayer at dawn. Hindu temple bells in the mornings and evenings. Sikh devotional music drifting down the street.

My "Christian" family? We went to a different building on Sundays.

We were what I now recognize as nominal Christians. Like many families, we had faith but hadn't yet discovered its transforming power. My parents went to church because that's what we'd always done—it was identity more than passion. We'd arrive at the church near our house, sing hymns, hear a sermon that rarely challenged anyone, then go home. Monday through Saturday, our lives were far from what the Bible offered us.

I was seven years old the first time I fell asleep during a sermon and woke up thinking about the game of cricket instead of Jesus. My Hindu friend never fell asleep during *puja*—worship. He stood there, hands folded, while his mother chanted prayers. I asked him once if it was boring. He looked at me like I'd asked if breathing was boring.

Here's what struck me as a child: many of my friends' families took their religions seriously. Hindu families kept shrines at home where mothers lit incense with sincere devotion every morning and evening. Muslim families prayed five times a day without fail. During Ramadan, even the children fasted with remarkable discipline. Sikh families regularly attended the *gurdwara* and spoke about *seva*—serving others —like it was the most important thing in the world.

And in our family? We sang about a living God, about Jesus who conquered death, about a Savior present with us, but our daily lives didn't always reflect the vibrancy of that belief. Some of my non-Christian friends seemed more committed to their faith than we were to ours.

In my years of traveling and preaching, I've met countless Christians whose faith burns bright—who sacrifice, serve, and love with abandon. I've seen believers who radiate the presence of Christ, whose lives are undeniable testimonies to resurrection power. But too often, these are the exceptions rather than the rule.

But as a child, this paradox puzzled me: **why do those who worship dead gods and prophets sometimes live like their faith is more alive than we who worship the living God?**

MY STORY: WHEN THIS QUESTION BECAME PERSONAL

All these observations from my childhood kept leading me back to one haunting question: Why does the resurrection matter so much? For me, this wasn't just theology. It was about an unanswered question about my own father.

Let me tell you why this question isn't just theological for me. It's deeply personal.

When I was seven, my mother made a decision that changed everything for our family. We started attending a different church in another part of town. The difference was striking. People actually seemed to believe what they were singing. They raised their hands. Some cried. Some laughed. The pastor preached like the Bible was urgent and alive. Over time, something began to stir in me. Maybe Jesus really was alive—not just a historical figure, but real and present.

Now I have had the experience of two churches, different expressions of worship, different ways to present the Word, poles apart. And my little naive mind was not able to come to terms with the question that bothered me: was Jesus dead or alive?

From the previous church experience, He seemed dead. In my new church experience, He was alive.

Then came February 22, 1990. I was nine years old.

My father was ready with his travel bag. "I'm going to Nepal," he told us, then smiled. "When I get back, I'll bring you a color television and a video game."

We didn't have much, so this promise felt like a treasure.

My siblings and I talked about nothing else for two days. He was supposed to return in a couple of days. He'd been to Nepal several times before for work. This was routine.

But he didn't come back.

Not the next day. Not the day after that. Days bled into weeks, then months, then years. *Until the day I am writing this—over thirty-five years later—our father has not come back.*

Just gone. No phone call. No letter. No explanation. One evening he was there, promising us a television and a video game. The next, he was a memory we couldn't make sense of. To this day, I still don't know if he is alive or dead.

Over the years, people claimed to know what happened. Some said he got in an accident. Others whispered about debts or trouble. Some said he was killed that night. Every story was different. Every story was speculation. The only certainty was uncertainty.

Here's what I realized: For many years, I could never settle with my father's disappearance. The not-knowing consumed me. Was he alive somewhere? Was he dead? Should I grieve? Should I hope? I lived suspended between impossible emotions, with an unanswered question burning in my chest.

The uncertainty was slower, more suffocating than grief. At least a grave gives you somewhere to stand. But disappearance? Disappearance gives you nothing but questions that never stop echoing.

My mother and siblings would pray for my father to come back. By this time, I had started to believe that Jesus is a living God, so my faith was that God would bring my father back and restore our joy. But nothing happened. I began to wonder if our prayers were vanishing into the silence, as though we were speaking to a God who could no longer hear us.

It brought me to question myself, **why would I settle for a dead god?** If I couldn't make peace with not knowing about my earthly father, so how could I worship a God whose resurrection was just a story, a hope, a maybe? I couldn't. I wouldn't. If Jesus was dead, if He stayed in that tomb like every other religious leader, then Christianity offered me nothing I didn't already have: another absent father, another unanswered question, another grave to wonder about.

But if Jesus was alive—truly, actually, historically alive—then everything changed.

THE NIGHT OF TRANSFORMATION

My mother suddenly had to raise three children alone. She worked long shifts as a nurse at the hospital, coming home exhausted. Money grew tight. School fees were delayed. But harder than poverty was the uncertainty. No closure. No answers. Just silence.

Yet in those years, church became essential to me. I felt God's presence in every service, and for a few hours each week, life felt like it meant more than survival. In worship, I could glimpse hope beyond the endless questions.

Then one night, I encountered the Holy Spirit for the first time, and it changed everything—inside me and around me. Our church held *"an all-night prayer service,"* and somehow it got me excited. I had never been in a service like that, so I wanted to witness this experience. I remember it was the month of August, monsoon season in northern India. It was raining hard, but my friend Peter, who lived in the same neighborhood, and I had decided that no matter how hard it rains, we would go to this prayer meeting.

Peter gave me a ride on his bicycle, and we both packed extra clothes and a towel and arrived soaking wet at the church. We changed, then went to the room where this prayer meeting was supposed to happen. The room had about fifty people.

We worshipped, and our pastor spoke a Word to encourage everyone to pray. Soon after, we started taking turns to pray. I have to be very honest here; I was scared to death to pray in public like this. We were seated in a circle, and it was my time to pray. Not a very impressive prayer, but deep within my heart, I prayed to God to show me that He is real.

It was at the breaking of dawn after a powerful night of prayer that the Pastor invited anyone who wanted to be filled with the Holy Spirit to come to the middle. I immediately knew I had to go. I did, and in a few minutes I felt a touch from God. A touch I had never experienced before.

My prayer was heard, did not fall on deaf ears. The living God filled me with the Holy Spirit. I felt alive from within; something shifted inside of me. I can still remember that night as if it happened yesterday. Jesus revealed Himself to me for the first time. I repented of my sins and surrendered my life completely to Him. From that moment on, He became *alive for me* and, more importantly, *alive in me.* That experience has never left me.

THE CHURCH THAT PROVED IT IS POSSIBLE

I want to share a beautiful part of my life that God blessed me with. I had the honor to plant our first church in Chandigarh with a friend of mine who came from a Hindu background. At our launch, there were probably about two hundred and fifty people in attendance. It was on a Tuesday night, awkward when I think of it now. So we had to wait a few days for our first Sunday service.

Our first Sunday service had a decent turnout. We started meeting weekly and also in the homes of people during the week for small groups. Then, a couple of months later, there was a sudden rise in the number of people from Hindu and Sikh backgrounds who started attending our church. People who'd never been in a church.

Even though we had Christians coming, soon these people from other religious backgrounds became a majority in our church. It was beautiful and shocking at the same time. I had been preaching about reaching the lost, and now we were reaching the lost in reality.

I watched these people transform. They took water baptism, going against their society, their culture, everything they'd known. Some left their families. Some were called "Rice Bag Christians"—the Indian insult for supposedly converting for money. As a matter of fact, it's considered the highest form of insult to a person who has accepted Jesus as Lord and Savior. ***I have never met a single person who converted to Christianity for money***. It has become very dangerous to convert in India now. There are several states where conversion is banned. These people face real persecution. Real rejection. Real cost.

There was a woman who used to worship with us every

Sunday, always arriving with her two young sons. One afternoon, after the service, I learned a truth that stunned me: her husband beats her every single Sunday for choosing to come to church. Every Sunday. Still, she came. There was even a night when he stumbled home drunk and threw her and the boys out of the house just before midnight. Yet at dawn, there she was—standing in the sanctuary with her children, joy in her heart and smiles on their faces. Jesus meant everything to them.

And here's what humbled me: there were people like her—people whose passion, commitment, and unwavering faith put many of us to shame, myself included at times.

They were coming from worshipping dead gods to worshipping a living God. And they lived like they believed it. Their transformation challenged me: if new believers could live with such radical devotion, what was stopping the rest of us?

All of it—from watching devoted Hindus, Muslims, and Sikhs as a child, to seeing varying levels of commitment in several countries, to witnessing new believers risk everything—led me back to one question.

Would you still be a Christian if Jesus never rose from the dead?

And if your answer is no and your faith would not survive without the resurrection, then let your life gently yet honestly reveal whether you are truly living in the light of that reality.

The greatest proof that Jesus is alive wasn't found in a bestselling book; it was found in the radical devotion of former Hindus and Sikhs in our new church plant.

WHY I NAMED THIS BOOK "THE DEAD JESUS"?

When I started working on this book, I asked over one hundred pastors what they thought about the title: *The Dead Jesus.*

Most said: "It's thought-provoking."

Some were uncomfortable. A few suggested alternatives. One pastor said, 'It makes me nervous, but maybe that's the point.' Another admitted, 'I don't like it, but I can't stop thinking about it.'

That's exactly what I was hoping for. Because comfortable Christianity is killing us. We've become so familiar with resurrection that we've forgotten its revolutionary power. Sometimes we need to be disturbed into transformation.

It can be convicting. It can be indicting. It is a mirror that reflects not what we proclaim but how we live—and that reflection might not always be comfortable to see.

I used to sing "Christ the Lord is risen today" on Sunday and then live Monday through Saturday as if the tomb is still sealed, the stone is still in place, and the body is still wrapped in grave clothes.

So many of us quote the resurrection. But do we really live it? The dead Jesus is safe. He makes no demands. He threatens no comfort. He disrupts no schedule. He fits neatly into our Sunday routine and stays buried Monday through Saturday.

The living One? He overturns tables, calls us to sell everything, and commands us to take up our cross. He shows up in our workplace, our relationships, our bank accounts. He refuses to stay in the tomb of our convenience.

No wonder we keep Him buried. This book is my refusal to let us stay comfortable with a corpse.

But here's what gives me hope: throughout history, whenever Christians have truly grasped the reality of the resurrection, revival has followed. Lives have been transformed. Communities have been changed. The world has been turned upside down. It can happen again. It can happen with us.

If the title disturbs you, good. If it makes you uncomfortable, even better. Because the real tragedy isn't a book called 'The Dead Jesus'—it's those Christians living as if that's what we actually believe.

WHAT'S COMING NEXT: AN INVITATION TO JOURNEY TOGETHER

In the chapters that follow, I'm going to take you through the actual events that happened from the moment Jesus gave up His life on the cross to the moment the guards were bribed to lie about the resurrection in Matthew 28.

Each and every event has a real life incident that is connected to me and my family.

But here's what will grip you: the people who showed up during those three days. The mother who watched her son die, yet somehow found strength to stand. I'll tell you how this connects to my wife Supriya's story of nearly losing our son to a diagnosis that said 'impossible.'

The secret disciple who brought several pounds of myrrh and aloe. I will walk you down a Walmart aisle to show you what extravagant love looks like when hope seems dead.

Another secret disciple who finally found courage—but only after Jesus was dead. My sister, Jyoti's story of sacrificial courage when we had nothing will show you what stepping out for His church really costs.

The women who followed His dead body to the tomb and became the first witnesses of resurrection. My mother, Veena's story will show you what it means to follow when hope seems buried.

The Roman centurion who came to crucify a criminal, but left declaring, 'Surely this was the Son of God.' What did this hardened soldier recognize in His death that religious leaders missed in life?

The angel who came, rolled the stone, and just sat. You'll discover heavenly authority like never before—and why sometimes the most powerful thing heaven does is simply sit and rest.

The soldiers who took bribes to lie about the resurrection they witnessed firsthand. I'll challenge you to consider what truth you might be burying for the comfort of a lie.

Each person's response to the dead Jesus reveals something profound about how we should respond to the living body of Jesus today, His Church. In their stories, we'll find our own. In their struggles, we'll recognize our struggles. In their transformation, we'll discover our potential for transformation.

This book is about encountering the living Jesus—the one whose resurrection should change absolutely everything. The one who offers us the same power that raised Him from the dead.

By the end, you'll face the same choice they did: Will you leave Jesus safely buried in the tomb of a comfortable Christianity? Or will you let Him out to overturn your life?

A PERSONAL PLEA

Note to the reader: *There were mornings I stood at the pulpit preaching about the living God while feeling dead inside. Days when I quoted resurrection scriptures but lived like the tomb was still sealed. Throughout this journey, I'll share honestly about my own struggles and victories. We're in this together. I'm not writing as someone who has arrived but as someone who is still becoming. Every chapter is an invitation to go deeper, to live more fully, to embrace the revolutionary truth of the resurrection. Thank you for taking this journey with me.*

I've spent my life in church, in ministry, traveling, preaching, serving. I've seen remarkable faith and heartbreaking compromise. I've experienced seasons of spiritual fire and seasons of spiritual drought. The older I get, the more urgent this question becomes: ***Are we going to keep worshipping a dead Jesus with our lives while singing about a living one? Or are we going to let the resurrection transform us?***

The resurrection cannot remain just a doctrine we defend; it must become the undeniable reality we live. Right now, too often, our lives contradict our hymns, and that has to change.

But change doesn't come through condemnation. It comes through encounter. It comes when we truly grasp what happened in those three days. It comes when we understand that the same Spirit who raised Jesus from the dead lives in us.

Jesus died—for you, for me, for all of humanity. And because He was dead, truly dead, His resurrection carries power—available to us today.

I don't know what brought you to this book. Maybe you're standing in a bookstore, wondering if another Christian book will say anything new. Maybe you're desperate for resurrection in some area of your life. Maybe you've been singing about a living God while feeling dead inside. Wherever you are, this book is for you.

Will you join me in letting that truth transform not just our theology but our daily lives? Will you help me live like we truly believe He's alive? Because if we do—if we really live like Jesus conquered death and is alive right now—we might just see a revival like never before.

The moment Jesus died, the ground began to shake. The moment when everything hung in the balance. The moment when the earth itself couldn't stay silent. The moment when heaven seemed silent but was actually preparing the greatest victory in history.

That earthquake hasn't stopped. It's been rumbling for two thousand years, waiting to crack open every tomb we've sealed Him in—the tomb of our comfort, the tomb of our routine, the tomb of our silence.

The moment is here: are you ready to feel the ground shake?

Turn the page. Chapter 1 begins at
THE EARTHQUAKE

CHAPTER ONE
THE EARTHQUAKE

MY WIFE and I are expecting our second child. It is almost the fall of 2014. She's six months pregnant. We're pastoring a church in Chandigarh, India, and our families and friends are pumped up for us.

In India, learning a baby's sex during pregnancy is illegal under the PCPNDT Act of 1994, which aims to prevent female foeticide. So we didn't know. That unknown became an invitation to trust God with what He was about to bless us with.

But here's the thing about the unknown: We cannot fully understand why God doesn't reveal what we're about to go through and still expects us to trust Him. How many of us have been there, questioning, "Why God? Why me?"

Little did we know what lay ahead would shake us, attack our faith, hurt our ministry, and caused an earthquake in our lives like we'd never experienced before.

When Jesus died on the cross, the earth itself trembled. The ground convulsed beneath Roman soldiers and grieving disciples. Rocks split open. Tombs broke apart. All of creation responded to the death of its Creator.

To everyone watching, this earthquake seemed to confirm their worst fears—everything was falling apart, hope had died, God had abandoned them.

They didn't understand: the earthquake wasn't announcing defeat; it was announcing victory. The shaking wasn't destruction—it was revelation. The torn veil, the split rocks, the opened tombs—all of it was God tearing down every barrier between heaven and earth, declaring that death itself had been conquered.

I'm about to tell you about our earthquake. And just like that first earthquake at Calvary, ours looked like the end of everything. But God was just getting started.

THE WARNING SIGNS

One night, Supriya felt excruciating pain in her abdomen. She couldn't sit. She couldn't lie down. She couldn't find comfort in any position. I rushed her to the hospital, where medication finally helped her relax and sleep. The next morning, she felt better. By evening, she was fine. One more night for observation, then home.

These were the warning tremors—those subtle shifts that signal something massive is coming. We dismissed them. We hoped they were nothing.

A week later, the same pain. Back to the hospital. This time, scans.

. . .

I was in the room during the ultrasound. Forty-five minutes —the longest ultrasound of my life. The doctor said nothing, just asked a few questions. Then he called another doctor to confirm what he was seeing. Supriya lay there in pain, eyes closed. But I was watching the doctors, and I saw something in their eyes that made my blood run cold. In those forty-five minutes, time stood still. Each second stretched into eternity. Questions flooded my mind—questions I was afraid to voice, answers I wasn't sure I was ready to hear.

THE DIAGNOSIS

The doctor told me to come back that evening to collect the report and discuss it. I took Supriya home. While she rested, I prayed. Then I went back. The doctor was flabbergasted. "There's a lot of unusual growth in the uterus and stomach area. She needs to go to a hospital with better facilities." What was about to come was beyond my wildest dreams.

She was referred to the biggest, most advanced hospital in Chandigarh. Through connections with Christian staff there, we got a private room.

You need to understand something:

Government hospitals in India are so overcrowded that patients lie on stretchers, even on the floors. A private room was nothing short of a miracle.

Even as our world was beginning to shake, God's favor was evident.

. . .

THE TESTING

For days, they ran tests. Blood samples. Ultrasounds. CT scans. PET scans. Every day, more tests. I was frustrated. I wanted answers. Waiting was the hardest part.

Waiting is where faith is forged. It's easy to trust God when you have answers. But when you're suspended between the diagnosis and the prognosis, between the question and the answer—that's where you discover what you really believe about God.

THE DAY EVERYTHING SHATTERED

One day, a doctor called me to his office and gave me the shock of my life. Supriya has thirteen tumors. One on her uterus. One on her stomach that has damaged close to sixty percent of it, and 11 on her liver. It's cancer. It's spreading. It's a rare kind. They had no research available for this variant.

Then came the second bomb: "She has probably a couple of months to live, and the child inside the womb is as good as dead."

The earth shook.

My whole world shook. I crumbled like I'd never experienced before. The doctor kept talking, but he couldn't understand what I was going through. Supriya's face was in front of me. I couldn't imagine life without her. Sixty days or less, and she'd be gone. Adriel, our firstborn son, four-year-old—how would he react?

Just as the ground convulsed at Calvary when Christ breathed His last breath, my world fractured into a thousand pieces in that sterile doctor's office. The words "couple of months" and "child as good as dead" echoed in my mind like the cracking of rocks, the splitting of foundations, the shattering of everything I thought was solid and sure.

While I had to act composed, there was a storm beyond control happening inside me. My life was about to change. Our family was heartbroken. Our church was devastated.

In that moment of complete devastation, I couldn't feel God's nearness. But looking back now, I realize He was closer than He'd ever been. When your world is shaking, when everything solid becomes liquid beneath your feet— that's when God holds you up.

TWO WEEKS OF SILENT AGONY

The doctors hadn't informed Supriya about her diagnosis yet; I knew, our families knew, and a few people really close to us knew. For two weeks, Supriya had no idea what was wrong with her. I was terrified of how she'd react. I didn't want her to lose heart, lose hope, lose faith.

But God knew what He was doing. And He knew who Supriya is.

. . .

Carrying this knowledge alone felt like bearing a cross I wasn't strong enough to carry. How do you look into the eyes of the person you love most and smile, knowing what you know? How do you carry on normal conversations when your mind is screaming with fear?

Here's what I learned: God doesn't ask us to be strong enough. He asks us to be willing enough. Willing to trust Him even when we don't understand. Willing to believe He's good even when life isn't.

THE MOMENT SHE FOUND OUT

One day, a doctor came to visit Supriya in her room. I wasn't there—I was taking care of things at home. But my sister Jyoti was with her, having come to spend time with us during this difficult season.

The doctor mentioned chemotherapy. A few times. Then she left. Just like that. The word hung in the air. Supriya's mind started racing. Chemotherapy? Why? What did that mean? She turned to my sister, searching her face for answers.

And in that moment, my sister Jyoti made one of the most courageous decisions I've ever witnessed. She told Supriya the truth. "You have cancer."

Sometimes the truth needs to be spoken, even when it shatters. Sometimes love demands honesty, even when honesty breaks your heart. My sister could have deflected, could have said "wait for Norman," could have avoided the moment. But she knew—this was a moment that was supposed to happen. My sister called me and let me know what had happened.

I came to the hospital later that evening after picking up Adriel from school. I walked into the room knowing everything had changed in my absence. The moment I saw Supriya's face, I cannot explain that moment in words. She had tears streaming down her cheeks. She looked at me with devastation and relief —devastation at the news, relief that I was finally there.

She hugged me tightly. So tightly.

We stood there, wrapped in each other's arms, and everything froze. The sounds of the hospital faded away. Time suspended itself as we held each other in the reality of what we now both knew.

For the first time since I'd heard the diagnosis, I didn't have to carry this knowledge alone. We were in this together, and from this moment, we started to believe in unity.

THE IMPOSSIBLE CHOICE

When the doctors finally sat down with both of us, they laid out what they believed was the only option: terminate the pregnancy immediately so Supriya could receive chemotherapy. The oncologist, gynecologist, and surgeon—three specialists—presented a united front.

"*You're choosing two deaths instead of one*," the

oncologist said, his voice tight with professional frustration. "If you don't abort this baby now, we'll likely lose both mother and child."

Supriya sat on that hospital bed, seven months pregnant at this moment, having just been told her baby needed to die so she might live. The medical team had laid out our options with brutal clarity: terminate the pregnancy or risk losing them both. There was no middle ground in their minds. They scheduled the termination for the next morning.

THE NIGHT EVERYTHING CHANGED

That night was heavy—the kind of heavy where the air itself seems to press down on you. Usually, my mother or Supriya's mother would stay at the hospital during the nights, but that night, I stayed with her. We needed to be together, facing this impossible moment as one.

As we were praying, something shifted in that sterile hospital room. The presence of God came in—thick, tangible, undeniable. And then God spoke to me. Not in some mystical, hard-to-explain way. Clear words: "I have given you this child. It's a baby boy. Name him Andrew. Everything's going to be alright."

I immediately picked up my phone and Googled the meaning of Andrew. I was blown away; it means STRONG MAN. Goodness gracious, God calls him that. The doctors say he is as good as dead. But I had heard God. Friends, when you hear God speak, no one's opinion matters. The world may label you weak, unworthy, or dead, but none of that matters when God calls you strong, worthy, and alive. This revelation birthed a new level of faith.

I looked at Supriya. In her shy, meek voice—the same voice that had said "I do" at our wedding, the same voice that had processed the cancer diagnosis with such grace—she said something I'll never forget: "I don't care about my life. I will carry this child, and Jesus will take care of my son, and he will be born."

That night was the game changer. Something shifted inside us. God moved.

AGAINST MEDICAL ADVICE

The next morning, instead of a termination, I was signing papers—documents that essentially said we were going against medical advice, that we understood the risks, that we wouldn't hold the hospital responsible when things went wrong.

The doctors were furious with us. They kept on trying to convince us to terminate the child and warned us, "If this child is born—and that's a big if," one doctor told us, "he'll be as good as a dead piece of meat."

Those were his actual words. That's what medical science said our son would be. But Supriya had already made her decision when God spoke.

She believed it. She knew God had given us his name—Andrew. She had felt His presence in that room. Against all medical evidence, against all professional advice, against every natural instinct of self-preservation—she believed.

In a matter of a few days after discussing it with us, they

started Supriya on Imatinib (Gleevec) 400 mg, an anticancer medication. What we didn't fully grasp was that while it kills cancer cells, it also kills new cells. Our son Andrew—God had already given us his name—was entering his eighth month of development, when crucial growth happens.

Then, a couple of weeks later, came the moment of truth. They performed an ultrasound to find out that our son had grown in size, had a perfect heartbeat, and normal movements. This was huge for us. The kind of news you want to hear in a situation like this. Our faith grew leaps and bounds on that day, and we kept on believing.

Author's Note: *This is our family's story, not medical advice. If you're in a similar crisis, seek qualified medical care and pastoral counsel.*

THE MIRACLE BIRTH

Supriya went into labor on December 26th. Andrew was born—he had been surrounded by cancerous tumors in the womb for months, bathed in Imatinib that kills new cells, growing in a body the doctors said couldn't sustain him.

The same resurrection power that brought Jesus out of the tomb had brought Andrew safely through the womb. "If the Spirit of Him who raised Jesus from the dead dwells in you, He who raised Christ Jesus from the dead will also give life to your mortal bodies through His Spirit who dwells in you" (Romans 8:11, NASB).

I remember it clearly: the first time I saw Andrew. Tears

rolled down my cheeks, and my heart was full of thanksgiving. Supriya was still unconscious and was being operated on as the doctors recognized that they could potentially remove two big tumors from her uterus and stomach. So she had not seen Andrew. In the next chapter, I will take you on a new faith journey right from this labor room.

They immediately ran blood tests on Andrew. The entire medical team was watching, waiting to see how bad it would be.

The reports came back. **No cancer in his blood. None. Zero**. The doctors couldn't explain it. But we knew.

As I write this chapter, Andrew is ten years old and will be eleven by the time this book releases. He's a sharp kid with a mind that catches things most adults miss. He's becoming quite the drummer—filling our house with rhythms that remind us that his heartbeat itself is a miracle.

But what moves me most is watching him with his mother. He's always thinking of ways to help her, this boy who wasn't supposed to exist, constantly caring for the woman who risked everything to give him life. Every time I see them together, I'm reminded: The doctors said those words. God said he'd be Andrew. And Andrew is very much alive, a walking, talking, drumming testimony that when God speaks, His word carries more weight than any medical diagnosis.

The earthquake didn't just shake our world—it opened the tomb of impossibility and brought forth life.

. . .

WHAT THE EARTHQUAKE REVEALS

When the earth shook at Jesus' death, it tore open the temple veil. For centuries, that veil had separated humanity from God's presence. It took an earthquake to rip it down. It took the death of the Son of God to give us access to the Father.

Our earthquake revealed things too. The depth of our faith. The reality of God's power. The strength of our marriage. The authenticity of our church community. It tore away everything superficial and showed us what was real.

But most importantly, it revealed the resurrection power of Jesus Christ.

The same power that raised Christ from the dead was about to work in our lives. The same God who conquered death on that first Easter showed up in room after room of that hospital. The same Jesus who walked out of the tomb walked through our impossibility.

"See to it that you do not refuse Him who is speaking... His voice shook the earth then, but now He has promised, saying, 'YET ONCE MORE I WILL SHAKE NOT ONLY THE EARTH, BUT ALSO THE HEAVEN.' This expression, 'Yet once more,' denotes the removing of those things which can be shaken, as of created things, so that those things which cannot be shaken may remain.

Therefore, since we receive a kingdom which cannot be shaken, let us show gratitude, by which we may offer to God an acceptable service with reverence and awe" (Hebrews 12:26–28, NASB).

LIVING THROUGH YOUR EARTHQUAKE

Maybe you're in your own earthquake season right now. Your world is shaking. Your foundations are cracking. You can't see how anything good could possibly come from what you're going through.

Let me tell you what I learned:

1- God is closest when everything else is falling apart.

When you can't feel Him, when you can't hear Him, when it seems like He's abandoned you—that's when He's holding you the tightest. The earthquake doesn't push God away. It pushes away everything between you and God.

2- What looks like destruction is often preparation for revelation.

The earthquake at Calvary looked like the end. But God was tearing down every barrier between heaven and earth. He was making a way where there was no way. Your earthquake might be doing the same thing.

3- When God speaks over your impossibility, believe Him over every other voice.

The world may label you weak, unworthy, or finished. Medical reports may declare it hopeless. People may call it dead. But when God speaks a word over your situation, that's the only opinion that matters. Let God's declaration drown out every other diagnosis.

4- God gives you milestones in the middle of the miracle.

Don't expect to leap from crisis to complete resolution overnight. God often gives you glimpses of hope along the way—small victories, unexpected provisions, moments when you feel His presence. Don't despise these. They're God saying, "I'm still here. Keep believing. I'm not done yet."

5- Earthquakes reveal what resurrection power really means.

It's easy to believe in God's power when you're reading about it. It's another thing entirely to need that power to raise something dead back to life in your own situation. Our earthquake taught us that resurrection isn't just a historical event —it's a present reality.

THE CHALLENGE

Don't waste your earthquake.

When everything is shaking, when nothing makes sense, when you're standing in the ruins of what you thought your life would be—that's not the time to curse God. That's not the time to abandon your faith. That's not the time to give up.

That's the time to watch carefully. Because God is about to do something that only He can do.

The earthquake at Calvary preceded the resurrection. The shaking came before the victory. The darkness was temporary, but the dawn was eternal.

Your earthquake isn't the end of your story. It's just the chapter where God proves that He's still the God of the impossible.

Hold on. Keep believing.

Trust the process, even when you can't see the purpose.

The same God who raised Christ from the dead is about to show you what resurrection power looks like in your life. The earth is shaking. But God is not shaken. And when the dust settles, neither will you be—because the God who opens tombs specializes in bringing dead things back to life.

Even when doctors say it's impossible.

CHAPTER TWO

THE MOTHER AND HER SON

HOURS OF UNPLANNED SURGERY. That's exactly what Supriya went through.

The day was scheduled only for a C-section but turned into an eight-hour ordeal when doctors saw they could remove two tumors—one in her uterus, another that had damaged sixty percent of her stomach. While other mothers held their babies moments after birth, Supriya fought for her life on an operating table.

At 2:48 pm on December 26th, Andrew was born. But Supriya didn't see him. She couldn't. I want you to remember that time—2:48 pm—because I'll show you later how God signed His name on this miracle with those exact numbers.

THE LONGEST DAY

I dread remembering that day. I was hopeful but restless, excited but concerned, joyful but stressed. Emotions mixed with faith.

From the moment I walked her to the labor room until her surgery ended late that night, I remained standing, walking, praying. I'd slip away from the waiting room—where my mother, Supriya's mother, and a few faithful church leaders kept vigil—just to shed tears where no one could see.

My eyes kept looking toward the operating room, hoping to hear something about my wife. Every passing hour was killing me, making me more restless, even when an assistant nurse came out a couple of times to say the surgery was going well and Supriya was stable. I was desperate for it to be over.

Hours later, finally, the surgery was done. I was told to meet her in the recovery room. Most government hospitals in India don't have heating. When I saw Supriya, she was covered in multiple warm blankets with several tubes attached to her body. A portable heater sat next to her bed, but it hardly helped. What I saw horrified me. Her body was shaking violently from the cold to the point they had to bring another portable blower.

That night was brutal. But Jesus had given her new life. She was safe. She was stable. The next day, a nurse walked into the recovery room carrying our son wrapped in a blanket. The baby boy medical science said should be dead.

Supriya had been unconscious for hours. Now, weak and barely able to sit up, she was about to meet her son for the first time.

· · ·

ONE MOTHER, ONE SON, ONE SAVIOR

Here's what you need to understand: Andrew wasn't the only child God was trying to save that day.

Supriya—a daughter of God, a beloved child of the Father—needed saving just as desperately as the baby in her womb. The cancer destroying her stomach didn't care that she was a pastor's wife or a woman of faith. Death doesn't respect spiritual résumés.

God wasn't just fighting for one life in that hospital. He was fighting for two of His children.

And here's what amazes me most about my wife: from the moment we found out about the cancer, Supriya made a decision that would define everything that followed.

"My eyes must be on the Son of God," she told me that night in the hospital, her hand on her swollen belly, ***"not on my own son whom I'm carrying."***

Think about that. The night we decided to carry Andrew and refuse his termination, we realized something profound: this wasn't only about saving and birthing Andrew. It was also about Supriya. She needed care, nourishment, and protection as much as she wanted to give it to the child she was carrying.

Every maternal instinct screams to fixate on the baby. But Supriya understood something deeper: she couldn't be consumed with stress about her child. She made a choice to focus on Jesus. He would take care of both His children—the one in the womb and the one carrying him.

Many times, we make idols of situations, people, and circumstances we're going through. We focus on the need rather than the One who can fulfill that need.

"If I look at my son, I'll make decisions out of fear," she said. ***"If I look at the Son of God, I'll make decisions out of faith."*** Through every doctor's visit, every sleepless night of pain, every terrifying statistic—she kept her eyes on Jesus. Not on Andrew kicking in her womb. Not on the tumors growing alongside him. On Jesus.

The same Jesus who was fighting to save them both.

HOLY GROUND

The nurse gently placed Andrew next to her.

What happened next felt like standing on holy ground. It was as if Jesus Himself had walked into that hospital room to conduct a ceremony I'd read about but never understood until that moment.

The same Jesus who once said from a cross, "Woman, behold your son," was now saying to my wife, "Supriya, behold your son." She traced his tiny fingers. Counted his toes. Watched his chest rise and fall with healthy breaths. No deformities from the cancer medication. No damage from the tumors. Perfect.

Tears streamed down her face. "Thank you, Jesus," she whispered.

In that moment, something shifted in the room. This wasn't just a mother meeting her baby. Andrew was the miracle, yes—but Jesus was the Miracle Worker. The child she'd refused to make an idol had been preserved by the God she'd refused to stop worshiping.

Two of God's children—one brand new to the world, one

who'd walked with Him for years—both saved by the same Savior. And at that very moment, I understood Mary. In that moment, I could see glimpses of Mary in Supriya.

STANDING BY THE CROSS

"Therefore the soldiers did these things. But standing by the cross of Jesus were His mother, and His mother's sister, Mary the wife of Clopas, and Mary Magdalene. When Jesus then saw His mother, and the disciple whom He loved standing nearby, He said to His mother, 'Woman, behold, your son!' Then He said to the disciple, 'Behold, your mother!' From that hour the disciple took her into his own household." (John 19:25-27 NASB)

Supriya is the purest soul I know—and I say this with complete honesty, not merely because she is my wife. I struggled with why she had to go through cancer, a deadly one. She is the sweetest person, never gossips, always loving and caring. So why did God allow her to go through this? Why did He allow Mary to give birth to the Son of God and then see Him die such a brutal death?

Before I go further, I need to say this: I want to honor Mary. This woman was there— constantly, faithfully, courageously—through everything Jesus endured. When others fled, she stayed. When disciples scattered, she stood. From the manger to the cross, from His first breath to His last, Mary never abandoned her post as His mother.

But that moment in the hospital helped me understand what Mary was doing at Calvary. She was doing exactly what Supriya had done after finding out about cancer during her pregnancy—keeping her eyes on the Savior instead of her son.

For thirty-three years, Mary had been His protector. When Herod wanted to kill Jesus, she and Joseph fled to Egypt. When He was lost in Jerusalem, she searched until she found Him. She saved Him from hunger with food, from cold with clothing, from danger with her watchful care.

But now, at the cross, everything flipped. The protector couldn't protect. The provider couldn't provide. The mother who had saved Him from Herod couldn't save Him from the cross. More importantly, she couldn't save herself.

Mary needed saving just as much as anyone standing at that cross. The womb that carried the Savior needed the Savior. The woman who had nursed God as an infant needed God to sustain her as an adult. She wasn't there as the mother of the Messiah—she was there as a child of God watching her only hope of salvation die. Or so she thought.

THE DANGEROUS PRIVILEGE

If Mary had a spiritual résumé, it would be unmatched in human history:

- *Chosen by God above all women*
- *Visited by the angel Gabriel*
- *Overshadowed by the Holy Spirit*
- *Virgin mother of the Messiah*
- *The only person with Jesus from conception to crucifixion*

. . .

Moses met God in a burning bush; Mary carried God in her womb. David chased God's heart; Mary's heart beat in rhythm with His. Elijah was taken to heaven; Mary held Heaven in her arms.

Yet at the cross, Jesus calls her "Woman"—not "Mother."

Why?

Because Mary's greatest privilege was becoming her greatest danger. She could be so close to Jesus physically that she'd miss Him spiritually. *Proximity doesn't equal salvation. Familiarity doesn't equal faith.*

This happens more than we think. The Pharisees knew every Messianic prophecy but missed the Messiah standing before them. Judas walked with Jesus for three years but betrayed Him for silver. The people of Nazareth knew Jesus since childhood but couldn't believe the carpenter's son was Christ.

You can be in the room with Jesus and still miss Jesus.

Throughout His ministry, Jesus had been preparing Mary for this moment. At Cana, when she expected special treatment as His mother, He said, "Woman, what does that have to do with us?" (John 2:4 NASB). When someone blessed the womb that bore Him, He redirected: "On the contrary, blessed are those who hear the word of God and observe it" (Luke 11:27-28 NASB).

He wasn't dishonoring her. He was protecting her from the dangerous assumption that biology equals salvation. That carrying God in your womb means you don't need God in your heart. Mary needed saving. Not because she was sinful in some exceptional way, but because she was human in the most ordinary way. She was a child of God who needed her Father just like everyone else.

THE TRANSACTION THAT CHANGED EVERYTHING

So here at Calvary, in tremendous pain, using precious breath, Jesus conducts the most important adoption ceremony in history: "Woman, behold, your son!" "Behold, your mother!"

This wasn't just about Mary's living arrangements after Jesus died. This was about her eternal address. This was Jesus telling His mother: "You need to be saved just like everyone else."

Jesus was establishing a new family—the family of faith. In this family, Mary isn't the mother of God; she's a daughter of God. John isn't just the beloved disciple; he's Mary's new son by faith, not flesh. The relationship that matters isn't biological; it's theological.

John records: "From that hour the disciple took her into his own household" (John 19:27 NASB). Not "after Jesus died" but "from that hour." While Jesus still hung on the cross, breathing

His last breaths, the new family began. Mary's transition happened while the saving was taking place. Just as Supriya had learned not to hold too tight to the child she was carrying, Mary was learning to let go. One mother disciplining herself not to make her unborn child an idol, another releasing the Son she'd raised from being her identity.

Both women learning the same lesson: being close to Jesus doesn't mean you don't need Jesus. Even if you carried Him in your womb. Even if you're a child of God yourself. You still need saving.

THE LEVEL GROUND

If Mary needed a Savior, then everyone needs a Savior. No exceptions. No exemptions. No VIP entrance to heaven that bypasses the cross.

Look who else stood at Calvary:
    - Mary Magdalene, delivered from seven demons
    - Mary the wife of Clopas, just another follower
    - The Roman centurion who participated in the crucifixion
    - The thief dying for his crimes

They all needed what Mary needed: the blood being shed above them. The ground was level. The playing field was equal. The mother of Jesus and the murderer next to Jesus—both standing on the same ground, both needing the same grace.

We've created a Christian caste system without realizing its consequences—super-Christians at the top with dramatic testimonies and powerful gifts, good Christians in the middle who faithfully serve, struggling Christians below them with doubts and addictions, and sinners at the bottom.

Mary's story demolishes this hierarchy with a single word: "Woman." If the mother of Jesus stands level with everyone else at the foot of the cross, our spiritual ranking system is exposed as the lie it's always been.

The missionary who planted fifty churches needs Jesus just as desperately as someone walking into church for the first time. The prayer warrior and the prostitute stand on the same ground. Your grandmother's prayers, your mother's faith, your father's position— these are privileges, not salvation.

Supriya learned this in that hospital bed. As much as she loved the child in her womb, as much as she prayed for him, as much as she chose faith over fear—she couldn't save Andrew. Only Jesus could. And she couldn't save herself either. Only Jesus could.

Two children. One Savior. Level ground.

THE FREEDOM OF BEING ORDINARY

When Jesus called Mary "Woman," I believe there was freedom in it.

Finally, she could stop being "the chosen vessel" and just be a person who needed grace. She could stop carrying the weight of being the God-bearer and just be carried by God. She could stop being exceptional and embrace being loved as an ordinary child of the Father.

There's exhaustion in maintaining spiritual superiority. There's bondage in believing you're better than other believers.

But there's freedom—beautiful, oxygen-in-your-lungs freedom—in admitting you're just another sinner at the cross. Just another child who needs their Father.

This is the great reversal of the gospel. The mother becomes the daughter. The one who gave Him physical life receives spiritual life from Him. The one who taught Him to pray now prays in His name. The one who carried God now needs to be carried by God.

Mary wasn't less because of this. She was more. More free. More saved. More secure. Because her identity wasn't "mother of Jesus" anymore. It was "child of God."

GOD'S SIGNATURE

You want to know how God confirmed He hasn't forgotten what He did for Supriya and Andrew—His two children He fought to save?

. . .

In 2020, we bought land in India. In 2021, we built our house. *Can you guess our house number?* ***AG-248.***

Andrew Gray's initials. The exact time of his birth—2:48 pm. Every piece of mail we get there. Every document that bears our address. Every time we write our address. We're reminded: God was there at 2:48 pm when Andrew was born. He was there when Supriya was fighting for her life. He was there saving both His children. He's still here. He always will be.

We will never sell our house in India. It stands as a reminder for us and the generations to come: When you're a child of God, He doesn't just save you—He signs His work. He leaves His fingerprints. He makes sure you never forget that He fought for you. Both of you. All of you. Every child of His who needed saving.

WHAT THIS MEANS FOR YOU

Let me make this practical:

First, examine what you're trusting in. Your spiritual experiences? Religious heritage? Years of service? Theological knowledge? None of these save you. Only Jesus does. You're not saved because you're special. You're saved because He's merciful.

. . .

Second, embrace your common need. You're not a special category of Christian who needs less grace. You're a child of God, which means you need your Father desperately. You need the cross as desperately today as the first day you believed.

Third, stop trying to save yourself or others. You can't be anyone's savior—not even your own children's. Release that burden. Let Christ be Christ. Let the Savior do the saving.

Fourth, fix your eyes on Jesus, not on your circumstances, not on your children, not on your calling. Where you look determines how you live. Supriya kept her eyes on Jesus, not on the child she was carrying or the cancer she was fighting. That focus saved her life—physically and spiritually.

THE FINAL WORD

As Jesus breathed His last on that cross, Mary stood there transformed.

She'd arrived as the mother of Jesus; she left as His follower. She came as the one who gave Him life; she left as one who received life from Him. She came as someone exceptional; she left as someone saved. And here's the proof:

After the resurrection, when the disciples gathered in the upper room, Acts 1:14 tells us exactly who was there: "These all with one mind were continually devoting themselves to prayer, along with the women, and Mary the mother of Jesus, and with His brothers" (NASB).

Notice how Luke identifies her—"Mary the mother of Jesus." But notice what she's doing—praying with the disciples, waiting for the Holy Spirit just like everyone else.

She wasn't leading the prayer meeting because she was His mother. She wasn't given special revelation because she'd carried Him in her womb. She was simply there, with one mind, with the others, as a follower of the Son she had birthed.

The mother who could have claimed superiority was sitting as an equal. The woman who knew Jesus longer than anyone was waiting for the same Holy Spirit as those who'd known Him only three years. Mary had completed her transformation from mother to disciple, from the one who gave Him natural life to one who received spiritual life.

She proved what every child of God must learn: privilege doesn't equal salvation. Proximity doesn't equal security. You need saving no matter how close you've been to Jesus.

Mary proved it first at Calvary and confirmed it in the upper room.

Supriya proved it in that hospital room.

Two women. Two children of God. Both saved by the same Savior.

The womb that carried salvation needed salvation. The mother who birthed the Redeemer needed redemption. The woman focused on her Savior, not her son, because she understood: she wasn't the exception. She was a child who needed her Father.

Every mother who thinks her child is her purpose needs to hear this. Every child who thinks their heritage is their salvation needs to know this. Every believer who thinks their résumé makes them special needs to remember this.

The ground has always been level at Calvary. Mary was just the first to show us. Supriya was one more in a long line who've learned the same truth.

If the mother of God needs God, then pride is just a corpse that doesn't know it's dead.

CHAPTER THREE
NICODEM(US)

I'LL NEVER FORGET the moment I stepped off that plane at Los Angeles International Airport on March 31, 2004. Everything hit me at once—the noise, the crowds, the sheer scale of it all. I thought I knew big cities. I'd grown up in Lucknow, a city of 2.5 million people in India. But this? This was different.

The airport felt like a maze designed to swallow people whole. I kept getting turned around in endless hallways, wondering if I'd ever find my way out. And waiting for me were two faces that brought instant relief: Pastor Tyrone P. Jones and his son Tyrone Jr. They had come to pick me up and bring me to Yuma, AZ.

Pastor Jones had offered me the position of Youth Pastor at his church in Yuma during our annual convention in 2003. After much prayer, I had agreed. I knew my life was about to change drastically. While Pastor Jones carried himself with dignified authority, Tyrone Jr. had this infectious sense of humor that immediately put me at ease. In a world where everything felt foreign and intimidating, his laughter became my anchor, and within days, he became like a brother to me.

Coming to Yuma—population 85,000—after living in a city of 2.5 million people, I remember thinking, "Where are all the people?" I eagerly waited for Sunday just to see a bigger gathering at church. One of the first places I remember going was The Coffee Bean where Tyrone Jr. worked. It was a very popular spot in that era.

I met new people almost every day and learned about American culture. In the process, I discovered that Mexican food was what I was born to love. To this day, my first stop after reaching Yuma is Chile Pepper. Their Machaca Burrito hits the spot every time.

Pastor Jones had made arrangements for me to live with their family while I learned to drive and get adjusted to this new world. The Jones family made things easier for me, yet everything seemed impossibly complex—from understanding traffic lanes to choosing which octane of gasoline to put into my car. I found myself asking Tyrone Jr. about everything. He patiently answered every question with that characteristic grin, never once making me feel stupid.

I had failed my driving test while doing a 3-point turn. Tyrone Jr. found out about it and offered to teach me at the church parking lot. After a few hours of practice, I passed my driving test the very next day. His influence continued to grow in my life. One of my challenges was clothing. The clothes I had brought from India suddenly seemed woefully inadequate for American life, and I had no idea where to begin. That's when Tyrone Jr. stepped in with his typical enthusiasm. "Man, we need to get you some proper clothes," he announced. "I'm taking you shopping." With his own money, he bought me clothes—a gesture of kindness I will never forget.

Looking back now, I realize that Tyrone Jr. wasn't just helping me buy clothes—he was trying to help me find my place in American culture the only way he knew how. His generous heart wanted to share his world with me, and it didn't matter that I looked out of place; what mattered was his desire to help me belong.

Coming from a very poor family in India, I had never lived in an air-conditioned house, so I had no idea what constant air conditioning would do to my skin. Combined with the desert heat of Arizona—dry, relentless, and unforgiving—my skin began to crack and peel. I shared my situation with Tyrone Jr., and he realized I needed something to put on my skin: moisturizer, commonly known as lotion in America.

"We need to get you set up properly," Tyrone Jr. said with that same grin. "First stop—Walmart." When we reached the personal care section, Tyrone Jr. stopped in front of the moisturizer display, and my eyes widened in disbelief. Coming from India, where moisturizer came in small bottles, I stared at these massive bottles with genuine amazement. There were 32-ounce bottles, some even larger, filled with creamy white lotion. "Get the biggest one," Tyrone Jr. encouraged, grabbing an enormous bottle and placing it in our cart. I hesitated, my practical mindset kicking in. "I won't be able to finish all that," I protested. "It's too much. This smaller bottle should be more than enough."

Tyrone Jr. laughed, but he didn't push. I selected what seemed like a reasonable size. "Trust me," he said with a knowing smile, "you're going to need more than you think." Within three weeks, my "more than enough" bottle was already completely empty. The Arizona sun and the air conditioner showed no mercy. So there I was, back at Walmart just three weeks later, this time grabbing not one, but two of those giant bottles Tyrone Jr. had tried to get me to buy.

Standing in that same aisle, I had to laugh at myself—here I was, the grounded Indian guy who thought he knew what "enough" looked like, loading up my basket like I was preparing for a moisturizer apocalypse. This experience became more than just a lesson about desert living. It became a profound metaphor for something much deeper—something that would revolutionize how I understood generosity, love, and what it truly means to serve the Body of Christ.

That day in Walmart taught me something I couldn't shake: sometimes, what feels like too much is exactly what's needed. Many years later, I found myself drawn to a story I had read many times before. When I read about Nicodemus and his hundred pounds of burial spices, everything suddenly made sense. He had grasped a truth long before I did—and at a far deeper level than moisturizer bottles and desert survival. He understood that when it comes to honoring Jesus, there is no such thing as "too much."

THE BOLD DECLARATION

There's something about Nicodemus that has always captivated me. He is the cautious outsider, the secret seeker who's afraid of what following Jesus might cost. Here was someone who initially approached Jesus under the cover of darkness, terrified of what association with this controversial rabbi might mean for his reputation and position on the Sanhedrin. Yet by the end of the Gospel narrative, when even the boldest of Jesus' followers had scattered in fear, it's Nicodemus who steps boldly out of the shadows with an offering that still takes my breath away.

"Nicodemus, who had first come to Him by night, also came, bringing a mixture of myrrh and aloes, about a hundred pounds weight" (John 19:39, NASB).

One hundred pounds.
Let that number sink in for a moment.

The typical amount of spices used for burial anointing was perhaps a few pounds— enough to honor the deceased and provide the necessary preservation. Nicodemus brought one hundred pounds. This wasn't just generous; it was extravagant to the point of seeming wasteful. It was enough spices to bury royalty, enough to anoint dozens of bodies, enough to make even the wealthy merchants of Jerusalem raise their eyebrows in astonishment.

Myrrh and aloes were incredibly expensive—imported from distant lands at great cost. Together, these spices repre-sented not just a significant financial investment, but a declaration of love that transcended all reasonable boundaries. Nicodemus had learned something that I was just beginning to understand in that Walmart aisle: sometimes, what seems like "more than enough" is actually exactly what's needed.

BEYOND REASONABLE BOUNDARIES

When I think about Nicodemus arriving at the tomb with his extravagant offering, I'm reminded of the criticism that often accompanies such generosity. "It's too much," the voices whisper. "It's wasteful. Surely something smaller would suffice." These are the same voices that echoed in my heart as I stood before those moisturizer bottles, choosing practicality over abundance.

But Nicodemus understood something profound: love cannot be measured by the standards of mere sufficiency. True love always operates in the realm of "too much." It gives more than is asked, serves beyond what is required, and loves past the point of reason.

Consider the context of Nicodemus's gift. Jesus was dead. The religious establishment had rejected him, his disciples had fled, and his mission appeared to have ended in failure. But there's more. By Jewish law, "The one who touches the corpse of any person shall be unclean for seven days" (Numbers 19:11, NASB).

During Passover week, this would have made Nicodemus ceremonially unclean, preventing him from participating in temple worship and the Passover feast. As a member of the Sanhedrin, his absence would be noticed and questioned.

Yet Nicodemus chose this moment to step out of the shadows and declare that Jesus was worthy of honor beyond measure. His hundred pounds of myrrh and aloes was a prophetic declaration—an investment in a future he couldn't yet see, a statement of faith when there was nothing left to believe, and an act of worship when the object of that worship lay silent in death.

And here's the beautiful irony: Nicodemus was responding to extravagance with extravagance. Years earlier, when he had come to Jesus by night, Jesus had spoken: "For God so loved the world, that He gave His only begotten Son, that whoever believes in Him shall not perish, but have eternal life" (John 3:16, NASB). God's gift was extravagant beyond measure—His only Son. Now Nicodemus was learning to give like the God he served.

THE LIVING CHURCH'S COMMISSION

As I reflect on Nicodemus's extravagant love and my own journey from scarcity thinking to understanding abundance, I can't escape a question that grips me—a question that every follower of Christ must eventually face:

What are we actually bringing to the living Body of Christ?

Not what we intend to bring or wish we could bring. But what are we actually contributing—right now, today—to the

Body of our Risen King? We are called to be the hands and feet of Jesus in this world. But too often, we approach this sacred calling with the same practical mindset I brought to that moisturizer aisle— giving just enough to get by, contributing just enough to appear generous, loving just enough to fulfill our obligations. The living Body of Christ doesn't need our leftovers. It doesn't need our reasonable contributions or carefully calculated offerings. It deserves our hundred pounds of myrrh and aloes. It needs our lavish, unreasonable, overwhelming love.

I have come to believe that each of us must honestly answer this question:

Are we a nourishment to the Body of Christ, or are we a punishment?

By punishment, I mean the ways we can wound, discourage, or hinder others— sometimes without even realizing it. Harsh words, careless criticism, pride, selfishness, or a stubborn refusal to walk in love can all be instruments of harm. Like a rusty knife, we can cut where healing is needed. But God calls us higher. He desires that we become instruments of nourishment—people who encourage, restore, and bring life.

The question is simple but crucial: Are we intentionally participating in God's redemptive work in the lives of others, or are we leaving unnecessary wounds in our wake? God's vision is for His people to move from being a source of pain to a source of blessing— from sandpaper that grates to oil that soothes. We may stumble, we may wound, but our calling is to become nourishment. The choice is ours—and the impact is eternal. When we gather for worship, do we bring energy and enthusiasm that nourishes the spiritual atmosphere, or do we drain the room with negativity? When we serve in ministry, do we give generously of our time and talents, or do we grudgingly fulfill our duties? When we interact with fellow believers, do we speak words that build up, or do we spread gossip and criticism?

Are we like Nicodemus, stepping forward with offerings that exceed all reasonable expectations? Or are we among those who watch from the shadows, calculating the cost?

THE EXTRAVAGANCE OF THE GOSPEL

The Gospel itself is a story of divine abundance. God didn't send just any messenger—He sent His only Son. Jesus didn't die a comfortable death—He endured crucifixion. The Holy Spirit wasn't given to a select few—He was poured out on all flesh. At every turn, God's love operates in the realm of "too much." Consider the feeding of the five thousand: "they all ate and were satisfied, and they picked up what was left over of the broken pieces, twelve full baskets" (Matthew 14:20, NASB). When Jesus turned water into wine at Cana, He produced the finest wine in abundance (John 2:6-10). When the prodigal son returned home, his father threw an over-the-top celebration that scandalized the elder brother (Luke 15:22-24, NASB).

This is the God we serve, and this is the standard He sets

for our love. We are called to be imitators of Christ—to love extravagantly, give abundantly, and serve beyond all reasonable boundaries.

THE CHALLENGE OF TITHING

Let me speak plainly about one practical way we can embody this principle of overflowing love: through our financial giving to the local church. Tithing—giving ten percent of our income to God's kingdom—is a spiritual discipline that trains our hearts in the ways of extravagance. It teaches us to trust God with our resources, to prioritize His kingdom over our comfort, and to invest in eternal purposes rather than temporary pleasures.

But here's what I want you to understand: ***tithing is not the ceiling of our giving; it's the floor. It's the starting point, not the destination***. When we truly grasp the Agape love that God has shown us, our giving becomes an act of worship rather than an obligation.

When you give to your local church, you're not funding an institution—you're fueling transformation. It's where the Body of Christ gathers, where lives are transformed, where the Gospel is proclaimed, where the hungry are fed, and the broken are healed. I challenge you to examine your giving. Are you offering the equivalent of my small bottle of moisturizer—just enough to appear generous while protecting yourself from real sacrifice? Or are you bringing your hundred pounds of myrrh and aloes—giving so abundantly that it makes others wonder about the source of your generosity?

. . .

OUR TRANSFORMATIVE CALLING

The beautiful thing about Nicodemus's story is the transformation we see from his first encounter with Jesus to his final act of love. When he first came to Jesus by night, he was cautious, questioning, afraid. But something happened in those encounters with Jesus. The teacher who spoke of being born again began to change Nicodemus from the inside out. By the time Jesus hung on the cross, Nicodemus had been transformed from a secret admirer into a bold declaration of Christ's worth.

This is what happens when we truly encounter the extravagant love of Christ. We cannot remain practical, calculated, and cautious. We become extravagant in return. We find ourselves giving more than seems reasonable, loving more than seems safe, and serving more than seems sustainable. The apostle Paul challenges us to "present your bodies a living and holy sacrifice, acceptable to God, which is your spiritual service of worship" (Romans 12:1, NASB). A sacrifice, by definition, costs us something significant. When Nicodemus brought his hundred pounds of myrrh and aloes, he was declaring that his resources, his reputation, and his very life belonged to Jesus.

We are called to the same kind of living sacrifice. We are called to bring our hundred pounds—whatever that looks like in our context. Maybe it's your time, freely given to serve in your local church. Maybe it's your talents, not only used for personal advancement but for building up God's people. Maybe it's your treasure, generously shared to support the

Gospel's mission. Whatever form it takes, our offering should be so generous, so extravagant, so beyond the realm of reason that it causes people to wonder about the source of our motivation. Like Nicodemus, our love for Christ should be evident not just in our words, but in our overwhelming acts of devotion.

THE ENCOURAGEMENT OF ABUNDANCE

As I close this chapter, I want to leave you not with guilt or condemnation, but with profound encouragement. The same Jesus who received Nicodemus's extravagant gift with gratitude is the one who promises: "And my God will supply all your needs according to His riches in glory in Christ Jesus" (Philippians 4:19, NASB).

God is not asking you to give from emptiness or to serve from exhaustion. He is inviting you into the joy of abundant living, where giving becomes a delight rather than a duty, where serving becomes a privilege rather than a burden, and where love flows naturally from hearts that have been overwhelmed by divine grace.

The church needs you—not the practical, cautious, calculated version of you, but the extravagant, generous, overwhelming version of you that emerges when you truly grasp how much Christ loves you.

The desert taught me that I needed more moisturizer than I thought. But life has taught me something far more precious: we all need more of Jesus than we think, and His living Body needs more of us than we're comfortable giving.

. . .

So here's my challenge to you:

Stop bringing sample sizes to a God-sized vision. Your King deserves your hundred pounds.

THE DAY JESUS DIED, His followers ran.

Peter, who had sworn he'd die before denying Christ, was hiding. John, the beloved disciple, had watched from a distance. The crowds who had waved palm branches five days earlier had screamed for crucifixion.

By Friday afternoon, the movement looked finished. The Teacher was dead. The mission was over. And anyone foolish enough to publicly align with the executed criminal from Nazareth was putting a target on their own back.

Which is precisely when Joseph of Arimathea decided to stop hiding.

For years, this wealthy member of the Sanhedrin had followed Jesus from the shadows— listening to the teachings, believing in his heart, but keeping his allegiance carefully concealed. He had too much to lose: his position on the ruling council, his reputation among the religious elite, his comfortable life. So he kept quiet. He voted with the majority. He played it safe.

Until the cross changed everything. Mark 15:43 (NASB)

tells us that "Joseph of Arimathea came, a prominent member of the Council, who himself was waiting for the kingdom of God; and he gathered up courage (*tolmēsas*) and went in before Pilate, and asked for the dead body of Jesus."

That Greek word *tolmēsas* doesn't mean he felt brave. It means he acted despite terror. It describes courage in the face of danger, daring that defies calculation. Joseph wasn't experiencing an absence of fear; he was overruling it.

He walked into Pilate's presence, the same Pilate who had just sentenced Jesus to death and asked for the body of a condemned man. In that single act, Joseph publicly identified himself with a crucified criminal. He torpedoed his career, his reputation, and possibly his life.

And then he did something even more remarkable. He gave Jesus his own tomb. Not a borrowed grave. Not a second-rate burial site. His personal tomb—the one he'd had hewn from rock, the expensive real estate he'd prepared for his own body.

Joseph gave Jesus the place he'd been saving for himself. The moment everyone else was running away from Jesus, Joseph ran toward Him— carrying grave clothes and a sacrifice.

A GOLD OFFERING IN INDIA

Two millennia later and thousands of miles away, I watched the same kind of courage surface in my own family.

We were poor in a way that's hard to explain to anyone who hasn't lived it. My mother worked at a local hospital, earning roughly eighty dollars a month to feed, clothe, and shelter three children. Every rupee was accounted for. There was no margin, no savings, no safety net. We had just enough —and some months, not quite that.

But we had church. And church was where we learned that following Jesus wasn't about what you had; it was about what you were willing to give.

One Sunday morning, our pastor made an announcement that stirred something in our household. A church under our spiritual covering had been evicted from their rented building. They needed help securing a new facility, and to raise the money, our congregation would be holding something called a "Gold Offering."

The gathering was set for a Thursday night so sister churches from the city and surrounding areas could join. The day also happened to be our pastor's birthday, and the only gift he desired was that we could raise enough money to buy land and build a church.

I'd read about gold offerings in Scripture. I'd never seen one. The very idea captured our imagination—gold, the precious metal that represents permanence and value, being collected to build a house of worship. That evening, my family gathered around our small table under a dim overhead bulb and talked about what we could contribute.

The conversation was short. My mother had no gold to give, so she decided she would contribute 1,000 rupees in cash—about twenty dollars at the time, a quarter of her monthly income. It was a significant sacrifice, and we all knew it.

I remember that this gold offering fell right in the middle of the month, and contributing one-fourth of my mother's income would have consequences for the rest of the month and beyond. But my sister had other plans.

THE ONLY GOLD WE OWNED

There was exactly one piece of gold in our possession: a pair of simple earrings that belonged to my sister. My mother had saved for months to buy them. They weren't elaborate or expensive by any standard, but in our family's economy, they were treasure. They were the only jewelry my sister owned— her one connection to something beautiful in a world that offered little luxury.

What made these earrings even more significant was a truth none of us spoke out loud: given our financial situation, we might never be able to buy gold again. This wasn't just jewelry. It was irreplaceable. So when my sister quietly announced, "I want to give my earrings," the room went still. I watched my mother's face. I expected hesitation, maybe an attempt to talk my sister out of it. Instead, I saw joy. Pure, uncomplicated joy.

"Good," she said. "Give them."

My mother had always been a giver—a faithful tither who understood that generosity wasn't about what remained after your needs were met; it was about trusting God with your needs in the first place. At this point, she had been tithing regularly for about four years despite her low income.

The night of the gold offering, our church hummed with anticipation. The faint scent of incense hung in the air as families filed in carrying jewelry, coins, and ornaments—treasures wrapped in handkerchiefs, tucked into purses, clasped in weathered hands.

Yellow packets were distributed throughout the sanctuary, and the rustle of paper envelopes mixed with whispered prayers. My mother held one in her hands. This moment never felt about money. This was about being part of something larger than ourselves.

When the time came, my sister removed her earrings. Without drama. Without tears. Without second-guessing. She placed them in the yellow packet alongside my mother's cash, and I heard the soft clink of gold meeting paper—a sound so small, yet it echoed something ancient. Together we walked to the altar. I was young. I didn't fully understand what I was witnessing.

But years later, the parallel hit me with stunning clarity: my sister had just done what Joseph of Arimathea did two thousand years earlier. She gave her most precious possession to honor Jesus—not from abundance, but from sacrifice.

Not because it was easy, but because some moments demand everything you have. Joseph gave Jesus a tomb. My sister gave God her only gold. Both gave what they couldn't replace.

THE COURAGE TO GIVE EVERYTHING

We often imagine courage as dramatic confrontation—standing up to persecutors, delivering bold speeches, marching into obvious danger. But the courage displayed by Joseph and my sister reveals something different: sometimes the most radical bravery is quiet surrender.

Joseph's tomb wasn't just valuable real estate. In Jewish culture, your burial site represented your final resting place, your connection to the land, your legacy. By offering it to Jesus, Joseph was saying, "The place I prepared for my own body? It's yours. Your honor matters more than my security—even in death."

My sister's earrings weren't just jewelry. They were her one claim to something beautiful in a world where beauty was rare. When she dropped them into that yellow packet, she was declaring that building God's house mattered more than her own adornment, that eternal work took precedence over personal treasure.

This kind of sacrifice transcends any single tradition. Every culture honors those who give beyond calculation—the parent who works multiple jobs so their child can have opportunities they never had, the stranger who risks their safety to help someone in danger, the ordinary person who surrenders comfort for a cause larger than themselves.

What makes Joseph and my sister remarkable isn't that they were religious. It's that they gave their best precisely when the outcome was most uncertain. Here's what makes both sacrifices so striking: neither knew the ending. Joseph buried Jesus believing the story was over. My sister gave her earrings to help a church that had just been evicted—a cause that looked desperate and uncertain. Both gave their best when the returns were invisible.

· · ·

That's where courage meets faith: the moment you give everything, not because you understand the outcome, but because you trust it matters.

BRINGING THE LIVING CHRIST HOME

Something shifted in my family the night we gave our offering. Walking back from that altar, we felt a connection we hadn't expected. That struggling congregation became our congregation. Their vision became our vision. Their future became tied to our sacrifice.

We had given away our only gold. And somehow, we had brought something home. Years have passed since that evening. The church that was evicted from their rented space didn't just find a new building—they flourished.

Today, they run a Bible college training students to take the gospel to Muslim and Hindu communities, some of the hardest mission fields on Earth. Every time I think about that ministry, I see my sister's earrings resting in a yellow packet. Our small sacrifice became part of something eternal.

The living Christ doesn't want to be buried in the tomb of your Sunday routine or hidden away like a secret you're ashamed of. He wants lordship over your Monday meetings, your Wednesday financial decisions, your Friday entertainment choices.

He wants to be at home in every room of your life. And making room for Him requires the same courage that moved Joseph to approach Pilate—a willingness to risk comfort, reputation, and security for the sake of honoring your King.

·   ·   ·

THE ULTIMATE SACRIFICE

Here's what we miss when we read about Joseph from a comfortable distance: this man gave Jesus his tomb during the three days when everyone thought the story was finished.

The disciples had scattered. The crowds had turned. The religious establishment had won. Every piece of evidence suggested that backing Jesus had been the worst investment in human history. And in that moment of apparent total loss, Joseph offered everything.

We're not called to give God our best when the cause is popular and the returns are obvious. We're called to give Him everything when it looks like we're throwing gold into a grave.

That church we supported with our 1,000 rupees and a pair of earrings? They were meeting in a rented space that had just been taken away. The cause looked desperate. The outcome looked uncertain. The sacrifice looked foolish.

But Joseph's tomb didn't stay occupied. Our gold offering didn't disappear into a failed cause. Because here's the truth that should arrest every secret disciple: when you give your best to Jesus—even when He appears dead, even when the cause looks lost, even when everyone else is walking away—you're not investing in defeat. You're preparing the place where resurrection happens.

Today, that evicted church is training dozens of students annually to carry the gospel to unreached regions. My sister's earrings became part of a movement multiplying disciples across some of the hardest soil on the planet. Joseph's tomb became the launching pad for the greatest comeback in history.

. . .

Joseph gave Jesus a tomb. Jesus gave him back an empty grave and a front-row seat to resurrection.

YOUR YELLOW PACKET MOMENT

The question isn't whether you'll face your yellow packet moment. You will. Every life contains crossroads where comfortable belief meets costly action—where you must decide whether to keep clutching your gold or place it on the altar.

What are you protecting? What tomb have you prepared for yourself that God might be asking you to surrender? What earrings—your security, your reputation, your carefully constructed plans—might become the seed of something eternal if you had the courage to let go?

Because here's the truth that should stop us cold: The tomb that holds what you're afraid to surrender is the exact place resurrection is waiting to happen. Your gold earrings might be funding the next generation of missionaries.

Your reputation that you're afraid to risk might be the testimony that brings someone to faith. Your comfort that you're unwilling to sacrifice might be the very thing blocking your breakthrough. The grave you give to Jesus becomes the ground where God raises what you thought was gone.

The yellow packet is being passed. What are you placing inside?

CHAPTER FIVE
LADIES FIRST

FEBRUARY 22, 1990. The date is etched in my memory like a scar that never quite fades. I was just a child, but I remember the excitement that filled our small house that day —and the crushing silence that followed. But this story doesn't end in darkness—God had redemption waiting, though it would take seventeen years to unfold.

My father was supposed to leave for Nepal for work, just for a couple of days like his previous trips. But this time was different. This time, he had made us a promise that sent us three kids into fits of excitement: he was going to try to bring back a colored television and a video game.

We already had a black and white television and an Atari console from one of his earlier trips, but a color television? Nobody in our entire neighborhood had one. We would be the envy of every kid on the block. I can still remember how we counted down the days until his return, how we talked endlessly about what it would be like to watch our favorite shows in color. We waited, watching for his familiar figure to come walking up the path. Two days passed. Then a week. Then a month. Then a year.

He never came home. It has been over thirty-five years since I saw my father.

To this day, I still don't know if my father is dead or alive. He simply vanished from our lives, leaving behind three confused children, a devastated wife, and questions that have never been answered. December 11th—his birthday—became a day of horror in our house instead of celebration. No cake, no songs, just the suffocating weight of absence.

My mother spent every resource trying to find him. She made phone calls, sent letters, reached out to anyone who might have information. But he was gone, and with him went not just our father but our financial security, our social standing, and our innocence. We plunged into a poverty so deep it felt like drowning.

The community around us began treating us differently. We weren't just the family whose father traveled for work anymore—we were the abandoned ones, the charity cases. The whispers followed us wherever we went.

I'll never forget the day that broke something inside me. I was playing outside when one of the neighborhood mothers called her boys away from us. "Don't play with them," she said, her voice dripping with disdain. "They're just cheap orphans."

Cheap orphans.

Those words hit me like a physical blow. I ran home with tears streaming down my face, my heart shattered by the cruelty of it. We weren't orphans by choice. We didn't ask for our father to disappear. We didn't choose this poverty, this shame, this label that seemed to follow us everywhere.

But here's what amazes me about my mother—even in the depths of that darkness, she never let us see her completely break. Yes, there were moments when I caught glimpses of her pain, when I heard her crying quietly in her room after she thought we were asleep, when I saw her staring out the window with that faraway look of someone searching for something that would never come.

But every single Sunday morning, without fail, she would wake us up with gentle determination. "Come on, children," she'd say, her voice steady despite everything, "we're going to church today." Her nursing salary at the local hospital brought in barely eighty dollars a month, but she never let our financial struggles keep us from worship.

She had one decent outfit—a simple, modest dress that became as familiar to me as her own face. Week after week, month after month, she wore that same dress to church. As a child, I felt the hot flush of embarrassment when I noticed other people noticing. She wore the same outfit for one full year.

The same people who had called us "cheap orphans" in our neighborhood were now watching us walk into God's house in the same clothes week after week. I wondered what they whispered about us. I wished we could blend in, wished we could escape the labels that seemed to follow us everywhere.

But my mother walked through those church doors every Sunday with her head held high, her hand gently guiding us forward, her voice joining in worship with a sincerity that came from a heart that had learned to cling to God when everything else had fallen away.

She wasn't there to impress the people. She was there to worship the God who had promised to be a father to the fatherless and a defender of widows. Looking back, I realize those Sundays were acts of defiance—not against people, but against despair. Against the voices that whispered we weren't worthy. Against the circumstances that screamed we should give up. Against the community that had labeled us "cheap orphans" and tried to make us believe we were somehow less valuable because our father disappeared.

THE FAITHFUL FOLLOWERS

Years later, as a pastor studying Scripture, when I began examining the women at the crucifixion, my heart nearly stopped. These women who stayed when everyone else scattered, who loved when love became dangerous, who remained faithful when faithfulness required everything—they weren't just biblical characters anymore.

They were my mother. They were every woman who has ever been abandoned yet chose to keep believing, who has ever been labeled and rejected yet continued to worship, who has ever walked into a room knowing they might be judged and walked in anyway because something greater than fear was calling them forward.

When we think of the crucifixion of Jesus, our minds often turn first to the dramatic events—the crown of thorns, the nails, the darkness that covered the land. We remember Peter's denial, Judas's betrayal, and the disciples who scattered in fear. But there is another story within this story, one of unwavering faithfulness in the face of unimaginable sorrow. It is the story of the women who stayed.

Allow me to introduce you to remarkable women whose love proved stronger than their fear, whose commitment ran deeper than their despair. These were not casual observers, but women who had invested their lives and resources in following Jesus.

Their presence at the cross was the natural culmination of journeys that had begun years earlier. In many ways, they remind me of women like my mother—ordinary women who display extraordinary faith when life demands everything of them. "Many women were there, watching from a distance. They had followed Jesus from Galilee to care for his needs. Among them were Mary Magdalene, Mary the mother of James and Joseph, and the mother of Zebedee's sons." — Matthew 27:55-56 (NASB)

THE CONVERGENCE AT CALVARY

As these women stood together at Golgotha, their stories converged into a single testimony of faith, love, and commitment. While the male disciples had fled in fear, these women remained. Matthew notes that they were "watching from a distance"—not by choice, but because Roman guards prevented closer approach. Yet even at a distance, their presence was an act of extraordinary bravery.

Their presence at the cross wasn't passive observation—it was active resistance against fear and social pressure. To be associated with a convicted criminal was dangerous. To remain loyal to someone condemned as an enemy of Rome could result in arrest. Being there meant being seen, being identified as followers of the crucified one. They chose presence over self-preservation.

Peter, who had boldly declared he would die with Jesus, denied him three times. The other disciples scattered when soldiers came to arrest Jesus. But these women stayed. From the moment of his arrest through the long hours of torture, through the agonizing climb to Golgotha, through the six hours of crucifixion—they remained. Their presence was their proclamation. When words failed and hope seemed crushed, their physical presence declared: "We will not abandon him. We will not pretend we never knew him. We will be here, whatever the cost."

YEARS OF FAITHFUL SERVICE AND FOLLOWING TO THE TOMB

Their presence at the cross was not a sudden act of courage—it was the culmination of years of faithful devotion. Matthew tells us they had "followed Jesus from Galilee to care for his needs." These were women who had been with Jesus from the beginning of his public ministry, possibly two to three years of consistent support.

Luke 8:1-3 tells us these women "were helping to support them out of their own means." They purchased food, arranged lodging, managed practical details that allowed Jesus and his disciples to focus on teaching and healing. While the disciples preached to crowds and witnessed miracles, these women were cooking meals, washing clothes, mending garments, managing supplies. They were doing the invisible labor that made everything else possible.

Their faithfulness was measured not in moments but in years. Through the popular days when crowds thronged to see Jesus, and through the growing opposition when religious leaders plotted against him. Through triumph and betrayal. They had given not just their resources but their lives to this ministry.

Even standing at the cross watching their Lord die, their instinct was still to serve. They watched carefully to see where Jesus' body would be laid. They went home to prepare spices and ointments for his burial. When Joseph of Arimathea took Jesus' broken form down from the cross and wrapped it in linen, these women followed. They needed to see exactly where he was placed, what still needed to be done.

Their vigil didn't end when Jesus breathed his last. These women followed the whole way through—from Galilee to Jerusalem, from the ministry to the cross, from the cross to the tomb. They saw it all. They were present for all of it. This is the nature of true faithfulness—it doesn't quit when things get difficult. It follows through to completion, even when completion looks like death and burial.

THE FIRST EVANGELISTS

What makes these women's story even more remarkable is what happened three days later. These same women who witnessed Jesus' death became the first witnesses of his resurrection. Mary Magdalene was the first person to see the risen

Christ. The women who had remained faithful through the crucifixion were entrusted with the greatest news in human history—that death had been defeated, that hope was not lost, that their Lord lived again.

They became the first evangelists, running to tell the disciples what they had seen. In a culture that often dismissed women's testimony as unreliable, God chose them to be the primary witnesses to the most significant event in human history. Their faithfulness at the cross had prepared them for their role as the initial bearers of the gospel message.

LEARNING FROM THEIR EXAMPLE

What can we learn from these remarkable women? As I reflect on their stories, I can't help but see striking parallels to my own mother's journey. These parallels aren't coincidental —they reveal the timeless nature of faithful Christian disci-pleship.

1- The Power of Longevity

These women had followed Jesus for years—through the entire span of his public ministry. Their faithfulness wasn't a flash of emotion but a sustained commitment that weathered every season, every challenge, every disappointment.

My mother's faithfulness mirrors this same longevity. It has been over thirty-five years since my father disappeared.

Years of questions without answers. Years of December 11ths that brought pain instead of celebration. Years of financial struggle, social stigma, and single parenthood. And through all of it—every single Sunday for over three decades—she has shown up to worship.

Like these women who followed from Galilee, my mother's commitment wasn't measured in moments but in years and decades. She followed through poverty, through shame, through the cruelty of those who called us "cheap orphans." Her faith wasn't a sprint; it was a marathon that she's still running today.

2-The Ministry of Provision

These women "supported them out of their own means," Luke tells us. They gave financially and practically to ensure Jesus and his disciples could continue their ministry. My mother understood this same principle despite limited resources. With barely enough to feed three children, she somehow still found ways to serve. She helped other struggling relatives when she could. She gave from her poverty, not from her abundance, embodying the truth that faithfulness isn't measured by the magnitude of our gifts but by the sincerity of our offering.

Like these women, my mother prioritized our spiritual formation even when physical provision was scarce. She showed us what it looks like to serve God faithfully regardless of circumstances.

. . .

3-The Witness of Presence

These women teach us the power of presence. The women at the cross couldn't stop the crucifixion or change the outcome. But they could be present—and their presence mattered profoundly.

My mother couldn't bring my father back or erase our poverty or silence the cruel voices that labeled us "cheap orphans." But she could be present—at church every Sunday, at our bedsides when we were sick, in our corner when the world felt overwhelming. Her consistent presence was her proclamation of faith.

Sometimes the most profound acts of faith are the simplest: to remain when others flee, to hope when circumstances counsel despair, to love when love demands everything. To show up, week after week, year after year, decade after decade, wearing the same dress but with the same unwavering commitment to worship the God who sees and provides.

4-Following Through to the End

The women at the cross didn't just show up for the popular moments. They followed all the way to the tomb. They prepared spices to return and complete the burial rites. They followed through to what appeared to be the bitter end. My mother has demonstrated this same follow-through. When others gave up on finding my father, she kept searching. When people wrote us off, she kept showing up at church.

When circumstances screamed that God had abandoned us, she kept teaching us to trust Him. She has followed through for thirty-five years and counting—through every valley, every hardship, every moment when giving up would have seemed reasonable.

A CALL TO MODERN WOMEN

Sisters in faith, when you face harsh realities—when your church goes through difficult seasons, when your faith is tested—remember these women. Remember my mother. Remember the women in your own life who have modeled unwavering faith in impossible circumstances.

Don't withdraw from the difficult moments. Don't let fear keep you from standing with Christ when standing is costly. The women at Calvary teach us that presence matters. Your presence in worship when you're grieving. Your presence in service when you're struggling. Just showing up— consistently, faithfully, year after year—is itself a powerful testimony.

They teach us that provision isn't about abundance but about faithfulness. Like these women who supported Jesus' ministry, like my mother who gave—you can provide for God's work with whatever resources you have. They teach us that longevity matters. In a culture that celebrates instant results, these women model the beauty of sustained, decades-long faithfulness. Your years of showing up, serving, remaining faithful—this is what builds the church, what raises godly children, what testifies that God is worth following even when He doesn't immediately deliver us from our circumstances.

My mother taught me that faithfulness isn't about having the perfect outfit for church— it's about showing up with the right heart. It's not about having all the answers—it's about trusting the One who does. It's not about avoiding hardship— it's about walking through it with grace and teaching your children to do the same.

The church today needs women who understand God's transforming grace and aren't afraid to share their testimony. We need women who serve faithfully in practical ways. And we need women like my mother—women who refuse to let circumstances dictate their commitment to Christ, who show up consistently even when they feel inadequate, who prioritize their children's spiritual formation over their own comfort. When your church faces scandal or division, when your spiritual journey leads through difficult terrain—stay. Be present.

Let your faithfulness be a testimony to others who are wavering. Remember that the women who witnessed the crucifixion were also the first to proclaim the resurrection. Your faithfulness through Friday prepares you to be a bearer of Sunday's good news. Your voice matters. Your witness counts. Your years of consistent, unglamorous service matter more than you know. Like these first-century women, like my mother in her simple dress walking into church with her head held high for over thirty-five years, you may find that your faithfulness through the darkness prepares you to be a bearer of hope and good news to others.

.   .   .

FROM CROSS TO THE RESURRECTION— GOD'S REDEMPTIVE POWER

The women at the cross established something beautiful: they showed that love is stronger than fear, that commitment runs deeper than comfort, and that faithfulness often requires nothing more—and nothing less—than simply being there when being there is difficult.

Their vigil at the cross was not the end of their story but preparation for their greatest moment. Because they remained faithful through Jesus' death, they were positioned to witness and proclaim his resurrection. Their sorrow was turned to joy, their mourning to celebration, their witness to triumph.

My mother's story follows a similar arc. The difficult year when she wore the same dress to church every Sunday, when she stretched her money to feed three children, when she chose faithfulness over comfort—they weren't the end of her story. They were preparation. ***Today, all three of her children serve the Lord along with their spouses and grandchildren.*** Her faithfulness through the darkness prepared her to be a bearer of hope and testimony to countless others who have walked similar paths.

And God, in His beautiful redemption, even restored what seemed forever broken.

December 11th—for seventeen years, that day had been a day of horror in our home, the day of my father's birthday that brought only pain and absence—God transformed it. In 2007, I found the love of my life, Supriya, who has now been my wife for seventeen years.

. . .

Her birthday is December 11th.

The same date that once represented abandonment now represents love. The day that brought sorrow now brings celebration. My father used to cook so well—it was one of his ways of showing love to our family. And God, in His kindness, gave me a wife who is also a wonderful cook, who nourishes our family with deep love and care.

Where there was loss, God brought provision. Where there was a day of mourning, God brought a day of joy. December 11th is no longer a day of horror for our family—it's a day of celebration, a testimony to God's redemptive power, a reminder that He can take our deepest pain and transform it into our greatest blessing.

This is what the women at the cross discovered on resurrection morning. Friday's sorrow became Sunday's joy. Death became life. Mourning became dancing. The God who redeemed their grief is the same God who redeemed December 11th for my family.

May their example—these biblical women and the modern women like my mother who echo their faith—inspire you to remain faithful in your own difficult moments. The same God who transformed these women and used them as the first evangelists is still transforming lives today. The same God who sustained my mother through years of single parenthood and financial struggle is still sustaining women who choose faith over fear.

Stand with them. Learn from them. Follow their example of faithful presence, whether you're wearing designer clothes or the same simple dress week after week. What matters isn't what you wear to church—it's that you show up with a heart ready to worship and serve. And be ready for God to use your faithfulness in ways you never imagined possible. The women at the cross became the first evangelists. My mother became a testimony of God's faithfulness to everyone who knew her story. Your faithfulness through difficult seasons may be exactly what someone else needs to see to believe that God is still good, still present, still worthy of trust.

The legacy continues through you.

CHAPTER SIX
WELCOME TO PUNJAB

LET me take you to the neighborhood where I grew up, where I played cricket with my friends, where my father disappeared, where we became the laughingstock of our surroundings and faced extreme shame due to the poverty that followed.

My mother was working at a hospital nearby and this house was an accommodation which the hospital had provided for us.

Punjab Nagar. "Punjab Neighborhood." That's what we called the area in Lucknow where we lived. Not the state of Punjab—just a place named after it. A neighborhood where a boy lost his father and didn't understand why.

Our poverty reached its lowest level when the hinges of the door of our bathroom broke beyond repair and we could not fix it, repair or replace it. We had no money to buy a new door and get it installed. The only solution was to hang a curtain and put clips on the side to keep us covered when inside. It was embarrassing—especially when we had guests.

The shame was real. But that same neighborhood is

where, years later, I accepted Jesus. In Punjab Nagar, I lost my earthly father and found my heavenly one. This is where God started the redemption of our family. When I moved to be the Youth Pastor in Arizona, I thought that was the end of my Punjab story.

It wasn't even the beginning.

WHEN GOD WRITES WITH GEOGRAPHY

While in Bible College, God had put on my heart to plant churches in Punjab and move to Chandigarh. He never gave me a timeline—then came the opportunity to come to America. My pastor was the one to initiate this move, so I knew that this is where God wants me in this season.

My time in America was some of the best years, friends became brothers, the unknown became familiar and Mexican food became my go-to.

Fast forward to 2006. I'm standing in Chandigarh, the capital city of Punjab. Not "Punjab Neighborhood" anymore. The actual Punjab, and God brought me to plant a church here.

I didn't choose Punjab. I didn't wake up one day and think, "You know what? I should move to the state my old neighborhood was named after." God chose it. God sent me there.

Every state of India has its own language, Punjab has Punjabi. I had no idea how to read, write or speak Punjabi. I still don't know how to read and write—I do understand some and speak only to make people laugh at me.

The first few people I met when I moved asked me to

learn Punjabi, I did not. When I look back, I think I should've. In spite of my limitation with language, God used me.

For seventeen years, I pastored in Punjab. We planted churches across that state. And then —because God apparently wasn't done writing His name across my life—He gave us our miracle son Andrew there.

The house we built in Punjab, where Supriya survived cancer during pregnancy, where we cried out for a child and God answered—that house became a monument to resurrection. But I still didn't understand the weight and magnitude of what God was doing until I heard the story that almost every Christian in Punjab knows.

The story of Sadhu Sundar Singh.

THE BOY WHO TRIED TO MURDER GOD

You can walk into any church in Punjab and mention his name—someone's eyes will light up.

"Oh, Sundar Singh! The Sikh boy who burned the Bible!"

That's not how they remember him now. In Punjab, they remember him as a saint, a sadhu, an apostle with bleeding feet. Sundar was fourteen years old, and his mother—the only person he truly loved—had just died. She was the one who taught him to pray, who took him to the Sikh temple, who showed him what devotion looked like. Now she was gone, and Sundar was drowning.

He went to a school founded by Presbyterian missionaries. They wouldn't stop talking about Jesus. According to

Sundar, he hated this weak, foreign, colonial god who got himself killed. Every day they read from the New Testament like it was supposed to mean something. Every day Sundar's rage grew hotter.

So one day, he decided to make a statement.

He gathered his classmates in the courtyard. He took a Gospel—Matthew or John, nobody knows which—and he started ripping out pages. One at a time. Slowly. Watching the words about light and life and resurrection curl up and turn to ash in the flames.

His classmates watched in silence. Some horrified. Some impressed. Sundar felt nothing but the emptiness where his mother used to be.

Good, he thought.

Let this foreign god burn.

That night, Sundar went to bed satisfied. But sleep didn't come. The next night was worse. He couldn't eat. Couldn't think. There was a weight on his chest, a voice in his head screaming: What if you're wrong? What if you just tried to murder God?

By the third night, Sundar had a plan. The morning train came through at 5:17 a.m. If no god—Sikh, Hindu, Christian, any god—revealed himself by then, Sundar would lie down on those tracks and end this.

TWENTY-SEVEN MINUTES BEFORE DEATH

3:00 a.m. Sundar wakes up. Two hours and seventeen minutes left.

He drops to his knees and prays. Not the memorized

prayers. Something raw: "O God, if there is a God, reveal yourself to me tonight. Because if you don't, I'm done."

One hour passes. Nothing. Another hour. Silence. 4:00 a.m. 4:30. 4:45. Pin drop silence.

Then at 4:50 a.m.—twenty-seven minutes before he planned to die—the room fills with light.

Not dawn. Not a lamp. Light that shouldn't exist. Bright and terrible and alive.

Sundar covers his face. He's terrified.

And then he sees Him.

A man standing in the light. And even though it makes no sense, even though this is the god he tried to burn three days ago, Sundar knows exactly who it is.

Jesus.

The voice comes in Sundar's own language: "How long will you persecute me? I died for you. I have given my life for you."

Then Jesus shows him His hands. Holes in the wrists where nails went through. Not healed over. Not hidden. The wounds are still there.

Sundar breaks. He falls to his knees sobbing. The peace that floods into him is so overwhelming he thinks it might kill him. The darkness that's been choking him for three days just... dissolves.

The light fades. Jesus is gone. But Sundar knows what just happened.

The dead god he tried to burn in that courtyard refused to stay dead in his bedroom.

. . .

THE PRICE OF FOLLOWING A LIVING GOD

When Sundar told his family the next morning that he was going to follow Jesus, that's exactly what they said: "You are dead to us."

His father performed a ritual—pouring water over Sundar's head to break the "Christian spell." It didn't work. Sundar was calm. Certain. Immovable.

They tried bribes. Money. Land. A future. Sundar didn't care. They tried threats. Disownment. Public shame. Sundar prepared for it.

The night before his baptism, someone put poison in his food. He got violently sick but survived. Later, he learned it was probably someone in his own family.

I've heard of families who poisoned their own children's food for choosing Christ. I've met people who survived it. One of my teachers at Bible college was chained and beaten because he started following Jesus, coming from a strict Muslim family. During my seventeen years in Punjab, Sundar's story wasn't history. It was Tuesday.

I've stood in the same kind of courtyard where Sundar burned that Bible. I've seen the same rage in families when their son or daughter chooses Jesus. I've been in a room where a mother pulled out a knife and tried to kill herself because her son, from a Hindu family, had accepted Jesus as Lord and Savior. I know the look in their eyes that says,"You are dead to us."

On his birthday in 1905, Sundar was baptized at a church in Simla. His father officially disowned him. The words were spoken in front of witnesses. In Sikh tradition, Sundar was now treated as if he had died.

Then came the hardest part. Sundar took scissors and cut off his *kesh*—his uncut long hair, the most visible sign of his Sikh identity. For a Sikh man, this is like cutting off your own limbs. His family watched and wailed.

To them, this was a funeral. Sundar Singh, the boy they knew, was dead. But Sundar knew something they didn't. He was more alive than he'd ever been.

WHEN LOSS BECOMES LEGACY

Here's what I realized walking those streets in Punjab: Sundar hated a dead Jesus. A foreign Jesus. A colonial Jesus. A powerless Jesus hanging on a missionary school wall. A Jesus who demanded he betray everything.

He tried burning that Jesus.

But the Jesus who showed up at 4:50 a.m. wasn't dead. He was alive. And He had the scars to prove He'd been dead and come back. Sundar spent the rest of his life barefoot in a saffron sadhu's robe, walking from village to village preaching one message: *"The Jesus I tried to burn refused to stay dead."*

He accepted Jesus in Punjab. Then he left Punjab and preached the Gospel across India, Tibet, Europe, Australia— everywhere. He owned nothing. Carried only a New Testament. Depended entirely on charity. He said, "I am not worthy to follow in the steps of my Lord, but like Him, I want no home, no possessions."

Over the years in Punjab, I met old men who shared his

story with me. Some had heard from their parents about him. His impact still ripples through generations.

What's amazing is that his father eventually became a Christian himself and started supporting Sundar's ministry.

In 1929, Sundar went to Tibet for the last time and was never seen again. He literally gave his life for the Gospel he once tried to destroy.

And I started seeing the pattern.

Sundar lost his mother in Punjab. I lost my father in Punjab Nagar.

Sundar accepted Jesus in Punjab. I accepted Jesus in Punjab Nagar.

Sundar left Punjab to preach the Gospel everywhere. I left Punjab Nagar to pastor churches in Punjab.

Sundar gave everything to follow Jesus. I became a father in Punjab—the place where God gave back more than I'd lost.

Two men. Same state. Same Jesus. A century apart. Same pattern of loss becoming legacy.

But before Sundar ever burned that New Testament, before I ever lost my father, there was another man who saw Jesus up close—and we don't know if it changed him at all.

THE MAN WITH BLOOD ON HIS HANDS

A Roman centurion. He didn't get a vision at 4:50 a.m. He didn't hear Jesus speak his name. But he had something else.

He had Jesus' blood on his hands. Literally.

This wasn't some distant observer. This was the officer in charge of the execution. Which means he was involved in every step: The scourging—flesh torn from Jesus' back with whips embedded with bone and metal.

The mocking—a crown of thorns pressed into His skull, soldiers spitting on Him, striking Him.

The walk to Golgotha—forcing a bleeding, broken man to carry His own cross. The nailing—you can't crucify someone "professionally" without being close enough to smell the blood.

Then the centurion sat there. Watching Jesus die. His soldiers gambling for Jesus' clothes. But something happened at that cross. Jesus said, "Father, forgive them; for they do not know what they are doing" (Luke 23:34, NASB).

Wait, what? This guy is forgiving the people torturing Him? The centurion had heard every possible response to crucifixion—begging, cursing, threats. But forgiveness? That was a first.

Jesus was talking to someone He called "Father" like they were having a normal conversation. In the middle of the worst torture imaginable, this man was having a chat with God.

The centurion couldn't help watching closer. The way Jesus spoke to the criminal hanging next to Him—offering paradise to a dying thief. The way He looked at His mother and made sure she'd be taken care of. The way He endured the pain without losing His dignity.

This wasn't normal. This wasn't human. Then at noon, the sky went black. Not an eclipse. Darkness that felt alive. For three hours. Jesus cried out, "My God, My God, why have You forsaken Me?" (Matthew 27:46, NASB). Then: "It is finished!" (John 19:30, NASB). Finally: "Father, into Your hands I commit My spirit" (Luke 23:46, NASB).

The moment Jesus died, the earth shook. A full earthquake. And the centurion—this man who had just tortured and killed an innocent man—looked up at the cross and said: "Truly this was the Son of God!" (Matthew 27:54, NASB). *He's declaring the divinity of someone he helped crucify.*

THE TERRIFYING SILENCE

Three Gospel writers—Matthew, Mark, and Luke—all recorded that moment. A Roman executioner recognizing Jesus as the Son of God. But here's what haunts me: not one of them tells us what happened next. Did he quit his job? Search for the disciples? Show up at Pentecost? Or did he just go home? File his report? Execute another criminal the next week?

The Bible is completely silent. And that silence is terrifying. I've had moments like the centurion. Standing at hospital beds where doctors said "impossible" and watching Jesus do it anyway. Watching believers in rented rooms worship with more passion than I'd seen in million-dollar megachurches.

Some days, all I have is recognizing that Jesus is real. That He's God. That He does what He says. But here's what we need to face: recognition alone isn't enough.

The centurion's story is powerful. His declaration is recorded in Scripture. But we have zero evidence that he took the next step. We don't know if he ever became a follower of Jesus.

And that's a sobering reality we all need to face. Because it means you can stand close enough to Jesus to have His blood on your uniform, declare Him the Son of God with your own mouth, and still walk away unchanged.

You see, recognizing truth isn't the same as surrendering to it. Declaring "This was the Son of God" is different from saying "Jesus is MY Lord." James puts it bluntly: "You believe that God is one. You do well; the demons also believe, and shudder" (James 2:19, NASB).

Even the demons recognize who Jesus is. Recognition without response and repentance is demonic theology.

The scary thing is how many people stop at recognition. They grow up in church, hear about Jesus their whole lives, can quote Scripture, maybe even declare with the centurion, "Truly this was the Son of God"—but they never truly repent and follow Him.

Jesus warned about this: "Not everyone who says to Me, 'Lord, Lord,' will enter the kingdom of heaven, but he who does the will of My Father who is in heaven will enter" (Matthew 7:21, NASB).

This is where Sundar's story becomes crucial. He didn't just recognize Jesus—he repented. He turned from everything he'd been and followed Jesus completely. The difference between recognition and transformation is repentance. It's the hinge that swings the door from knowing about Jesus to knowing Jesus.

So what made the difference for Sundar? When Jesus appeared to him, Sundar didn't just say, "Yes, you're the Son of God" and go back to bed. He fell to his knees. He surrendered. He counted the cost—family, reputation, comfort, safety—and said yes anyway. He didn't just recognize Jesus; he followed Him.

The centurion might be in heaven. I hope he is. But he might also be the most tragic character in the Gospels—the man who got it right and did nothing about it. I pastored in Punjab for seventeen years. I watched Sundar Singh's story transform people. But I also watched people who KNEW the truth—who could quote it, preach it, recognize it—and never let it cost them anything.

They had recognition without repentance. Knowledge without surrender. They saw Jesus clearly and walked away anyway.

Maybe you're reading this and you realize you've been living like the centurion— recognizing Jesus but never really following Him. You've been intellectually convinced but never spiritually converted. You know about Jesus, but you don't know Jesus. The beautiful thing is, it's not too late. Sundar was an enemy one night and a follower the next morning. The thief on the cross went from mocking Jesus to being promised paradise in a matter of hours. God can transform a life in a moment when someone genuinely repents and believes.

But here's what you need to understand: recognition is just the first step. Following Jesus requires more. It requires turning from sin (repentance), trusting in Christ alone for salvation (faith), and committing to follow Him no matter the cost (discipleship). That's what makes someone a guardian.

Not recognition alone, but recognition that leads to repentance, repentance that leads to following, and following that leads to protecting what you've been given.

WHICH STORY WILL BE YOURS?

If He can conquer a boy who tried to murder Him with fire, if He can make a Roman executioner declare His divinity with blood still on his hands, He can conquer whatever dead faith you're carrying today.

But you have to move beyond recognition. You have to repent. You have to follow. I repented in Punjab Nagar. Sundar repented in Punjab. Sundar lost everything and found everything. The centurion recognized truth and maybe walked away. I lost my father in Punjab Nagar—and God made me a father in Punjab. The Church doesn't need more spectators. It needs guardians. People who don't just recognize Jesus but follow Him so completely that they'll protect His truth and His people no matter the cost.

The centurion saw the Son of God and kept his sword. Sundar saw the Son of God and gave his life. Your move. The only question left is: Will you let Him take the scissors to everything you're still holding onto?

Recognition costs nothing. Repentance costs everything. That's why most people stop at recognition.

. . .

YOUR MOVE: BECOME A GUARDIAN

If you're still reading, you've already made a choice. Here's what it looks like to live it:

1-Guard Your Own Heart—You can't pour from an empty cup. If your prayer life is dry, if you're compromising, if you're letting bitterness take root—how can you protect others? Watch your life and doctrine closely. Life first, then doctrine.

2-Guard the Truth—Know your Bible well enough to recognize when something sounds off. Peter said, "but sanctify Christ as Lord in your hearts, always being ready to make a defense to everyone who asks you to give an account for the hope that is in you, yet with gentleness and reverence" (1 Peter 3:15, NASB).

3-Guard the People—Notice who's struggling. Who's new. Who's missing. Send a text. Make a phone call. Show up with a meal. Sometimes the most powerful ministry is just paying attention and showing you care. If you see abuse or serious problems, speak up and make sure proper authorities are notified.

4-Guard Unity—When you hear gossip, shut it down. When conflicts arise, be the voice of reconciliation. Support your church leadership when they make tough but necessary decisions. Churches fall apart faster from internal drama than from any outside attack.

You and I are centurions too. We've seen enough to recognize Him. Now we decide: walk away, or surrender.

CHAPTER SEVEN
THE SITTING ANGEL

MY WALLET WAS GONE.

I patted my back pocket again—empty. My stomach dropped. We were in the middle of Global Village in Dubai, surrounded by thousands of strangers from every corner of the world, and somewhere in this labyrinth of international pavilions, my wallet was missing. Our cash. Our cards. Everything.

My wife Supriya saw my face and knew immediately. Our boys, Adriel and three-year-old Andrew, sensed the shift in the air. We had been celebrating our tenth anniversary—a trip of a lifetime gifted by a generous friend. Seven days in Dubai, ten days in the Holy Land.

Our family was super excited about it. It was our first trip out of India as a family, and the anticipation had been building for months.

Everything about Dubai amazed us. From the Dubai Mall to the Burj Khalifa, from the Desert Safari to the Dhow Cruise, from the by lanes of the Gold Souk to the majesty of the desert. We had stepped into a man-made marvel, and I understood why people return again and again.

I usually don't let my wallet stay in my back pocket while I sit, so when I was tired from walking all day and found a place to rest, I took out my wallet and placed it next to me on a bench. After about ten minutes, we all got up and walked off to see different sections of the park.

About dinner time, I realized I didn't have my wallet. But because I remembered exactly where I had placed it—on a bench when I sat down to rest my aching feet—I told my family to wait. I ran. Back through the crowds, past the glittering pavilions, my heart pounding with every step.

I turned the corner—braced myself for the sight of an empty bench, or worse, someone casually walking away with it, but there it was.

My wallet. Sitting exactly where I'd left it. Untouched. In plain view. After hours in one of the most visited places on earth.

LAWS OF THE LAND

There was nothing special about my wallet. It wasn't locked. It wasn't hidden. It wasn't guarded by some invisible force field. Thousands of people had walked past it. Any one of them could have picked it up, pocketed it, disappeared into the crowd.

But no one touched it.

In Dubai, the laws are strict—incredibly strict. Theft, even of small items, carries severe penalties. Cameras are everywhere. Police presence is constant. But it's more than fear of punishment. There's a deep cultural respect for property, reinforced by law enforcement that's both visible and effective. Everyone—citizens and visitors alike—understands that the consequences of breaking the law are swift and certain.

What struck me wasn't just that my wallet was still there. I knew—without a shadow of doubt—that no one had touched it. It was in the same position I had kept it.

Not because people are inherently more honest in Dubai, but because there was an authority present. An understood order that makes certain things secure without anyone physically guarding them.

The authority of Dubai's laws had protected what I couldn't protect myself.

My panic turned to wonder. I stood there, staring at that wallet on the bench, and something shifted in my understanding of what it means for authority to be present.

I didn't know it yet, but I was about to see the same principle displayed on an infinitely grander scale.

THE EMPTY PLACE

A few days later, I stood with my family at the Garden Tomb in Jerusalem. One hand rested on Andrew's shoulder to keep him from wandering. My eyes traced the rough-hewn entrance cut into the rock face.

The stone was gone now, of course—rolled away two millennia ago. But standing there, I could almost see it. That massive wheel of rock, sealed with Roman authority, guarded by soldiers who had no idea they were standing watch over an empty assignment.

And then I saw him. Not with my eyes—with something deeper.

The angel.

Not hovering in mid-air. Not standing guard with a flaming sword. Not pacing nervously, waiting for instructions. Sitting. Calmly. Confidently. Right there on the very stone that was meant to seal death's victory.

"And behold, a severe earthquake had occurred, for an angel of the Lord descended from heaven and came and rolled away the stone and sat upon it." Matthew 28:2 (NASB)

His appearance like lightning. His clothing white as snow. And his posture—his posture —declaring a message louder than any words: *This is finished.*

We often picture the moment of resurrection like a battle —a furious, heaven-rending blast of power. An archangel with a sword of fire, guarding a precarious victory. Wings unfurled. Voice thundering.

But that's not what I saw.

The angel was sitting. Right there on the very stone that was meant to seal death's victory.

That visual gripped me and has never let go. It wasn't what the angel did—it was how he positioned himself afterward. The posture of rest. The posture of authority. The posture of a victory so complete that there was nothing left to do but take a seat.

And suddenly, standing in that garden with my family, the two images connected: my wallet sitting undisturbed on a bench in Dubai, and an angel sitting undisturbed on a stone outside an empty tomb.

Both remained secure not because someone was guarding them, but because of the authority present in that place.

WHEN HEAVEN SITS

Here's what unlocked everything for me about this angel.

There was nothing special about my wallet that kept people from touching it. It wasn't the wallet itself. It was the laws of the land—and everyone understanding the authority and consequence of that law being broken.

The same way, there was nothing special about the angel. He wasn't flexing supernatural muscle. He wasn't radiating terrifying power to ward off intruders. He was simply a display of heaven's law—***that when heaven decides to resurrect the King of Heaven, no one touches it.***

No one can stop it. No one dares interfere.

When heaven sits, it's because heaven has already spoken the final word. It's as if all of heaven was saying: This is done.

We're not here to help—we're here to honor.

THE MIRACLE THAT DIDN'T NEED HELP

For years I thought of miracles as moments when heaven steps in to fix what we cannot. But the resurrection of Jesus shattered that definition.

The greatest miracle in all creation didn't need help. It needed surrender. It didn't require an army of angels. It required a dying Savior.

"No one has taken it away from Me, but I lay it down on My own. I have authority to lay it down, and I have authority to take it back." John 10:18 (NASB)

The biggest miracle in history didn't need heaven's assistance—it needed Jesus to die.

That stops me cold. Because if heaven didn't need to help Jesus rise, *then what was the angel doing there?*

He was there as a witness. A presence. A heavenly acknowledgment that the power of life had already done its work.

And it makes me wonder: How many times have I expected God to show up and help, when in reality, He's already finished the work—and now He's simply sitting beside it, waiting for me to see?

HEAVEN'S STILLNESS, EARTH'S TREMBLING

When I read Matthew's account carefully, I notice something almost no one talks about— the stark contrast of reactions in that garden. "The guards shook from fear of him and became like dead men." Matthew 28:4 (NASB)

The ground is trembling. Roman soldiers—trained warriors who had seen blood and battle—are collapsing in terror. And heaven? Heaven sits. The quietest act in the midst of the most violent upheaval.

Remember Genesis 2:2: "By the seventh day God completed His work which He had done, and He rested." The same God who rested after creation now rests after redemption. *Heaven isn't anxious. Heaven isn't scrambling. Heaven is still because the work is done.* Divine presence doesn't always come to move mountains or stir chaos. Sometimes it comes to sit—to reign in calm authority over what once terrified us.

ROLLED AWAY FOR US

When the angel speaks to the women who arrive at dawn, his words are tender: "Do not be afraid; for I know that you are looking for Jesus who has been crucified. He is not here, for He has risen, just as He said. Come, see the place where He was lying." Matthew 28:5-6 (NASB)

He doesn't shout. He doesn't command. He invites. Come, see.

That's when I understood something that changed everything: the angel didn't roll away the stone to let Jesus out. He rolled it away to let us in.

After all, the resurrected Christ could pass through sealed doors. John tells us that "Jesus came, the doors having been shut, and stood in their midst" (John 20:26). He certainly didn't need a stone moved to exit a tomb.

The stone was rolled away for us—so we could witness the reality of what had already happened in the darkness.

Heaven didn't intervene to change the outcome. Heaven appeared to reveal it.

How often have I stood before a "stone"—something that looked final, hopeless, sealed— asking God to remove it? But sometimes, He rolls the stone away not to change what's behind it, but to show me that resurrection has already happened. The miracle I'm desperately seeking may have already occurred in the hidden places, blocked from view by something that looks like an ending.

The angel wasn't there to perform a miracle. He was there to uncover one.

WHEN TOMBSTONES BECOME THRONES

That visual of the angel sitting has never left me. The stone that once sealed death became a throne of rest.

Think about that transformation for a moment. The stone wasn't removed and discarded. It wasn't destroyed or thrown aside as refuse. It became something new. A seat of authority. A platform for proclamation. A throne from which heaven announces victory over death itself.

"The LORD says to my Lord: 'Sit at My right hand until I make Your enemies a footstool for Your feet.'" Psalm 110:1 (NASB)

I can almost see it—the radiant messenger, seated calmly in the breaking dawn, while the guards tremble at his feet. The same slab that represented despair now supports divine peace.

Death thought it had placed the final seal on Jesus's ministry. The authorities believed they had closed the chapter on this troublemaking rabbi from Nazareth. Instead, that very seal became the stage for the greatest announcement in human history.

The stone meant to keep Him in became the throne from which heaven declared He had risen.

This is what resurrection does. It doesn't just reverse death—it repurposes it. It takes what the enemy meant for harm and transforms it into a testimony of God's power.

Presence doesn't erase what happened; it transforms it. It turns graves into gardens, tombstones into thrones.

THROUGH, NOT AROUND

For so long, I thought resurrection was the miracle of power. Now I see it's the miracle of surrender. "Unless a grain of wheat falls into the earth and dies, it remains alone; but if it dies, it bears much fruit." John 12:24 (NASB)

The seed has no choice but to fall and die. Jesus had every choice—and chose it anyway. That's what makes the resurrection not just a miracle of power, but a miracle of love.

The victory wasn't in avoiding the grave—it was in entering it and undoing it from within. He didn't go around death. He went through it. And in going through it, He transformed it forever.

That changes how I see everything in my own life. The miracles I'm waiting for don't always require more power— sometimes they require my surrender. Maybe what looks like an ending isn't the absence of God, but the beginning of resurrection already at work beneath the surface.

I know this because I've lived it.

When Supriya was diagnosed with cancer, I paced around that tomb for months— begging God to intervene, to fix, to rescue. And when Andrew was in the womb, his life in danger threatening to take both him and his mother, we couldn't go around the crisis.

We had to go through it. Two potential deaths in our family, and all I could do was surrender what I couldn't control.

Those stones looked final. Sealed. Hopeless.

Maybe the stone that you're staring at—the impossible situation, the dead dream, the sealed hope—isn't there to block you. Maybe it's marking the exact spot where God is already bringing something dead back to life.

You just can't see it yet.

Because resurrection always happens in the dark first.

THE FIRST WITNESS

When the angel speaks, heaven becomes the first witness to resurrection: "Why are you seeking the living One among the dead? He is not here, but He has risen." Luke 24:5-6 (NASB)

It's as though heaven is saying: This is what we saw. This is what eternity already knew. Before the disciples understood, before the world believed, heaven was already seated beside the empty place. And that comforts me. Because it means even when I don't see the miracle yet—heaven does.

Heaven knows all about us. In spite of our sins that separated us from God, heaven still has us in mind—you and me both.

THE POSTURE OF PEACE

I've started noticing something about Scripture: God always sits after He's finished. After creation, He rested. After the cross, Jesus "sat down at the right hand of the Majesty on high" (Hebrews 1:3 NASB). And now, at the tomb, the angel sits.

Every time heaven sits, it's because heaven is at peace. That stone-seat outside the tomb is more than a detail—it's a declaration. The posture of heaven says: This is done.

Maybe that's the posture you need too. To stop pacing around your own tombs—the things you've buried in worry, fear, or shame—and simply sit beside them in the peace of what Christ has already accomplished.

I used to chase the power of God—the earthquakes, the signs, the breakthroughs. But this story taught me something: ***presence is greater than power.***

Power moves things. Presence transforms them. Power can roll away stones. Presence sits beside them in peace.

When I picture that angel on the stone, I no longer see an act of might—I see an image of confidence. Heaven doesn't need to prove anything; it simply reveals what's real.

COME AND SEE

"Come, see the place where He was lying." Matthew 28:6 (NASB)

The angel's invitation still echoes across two thousand years. He's not asking you to achieve anything. He's not commanding you to go build something or prove something or earn something. He's asking you to look. To see. To witness what has already happened.

Sometimes faith is less about doing and more about seeing. Less about achieving and more about receiving. Less about making something happen and more about recognizing what already has.

The empty tomb doesn't need my help. The resurrection doesn't require my effort. But it does ask for my attention.

It invites me to come and see—to look at the place where death claimed victory, and recognize that the victory was overturned. To stare into the darkness where Jesus lay, and see that the darkness is empty now, flooded with light.

So come. See the place where your fear was supposed to win—and notice it's empty now. And beside it, heaven sits. Calm. Confident. At rest.

Just like my wallet on that bench in Dubai—untouched, unguarded, yet completely secure. Not because anyone was watching. Because authority was present.

The work is finished. God is on the throne. Come and have a front row seat.

CHAPTER EIGHT
NOT FOR SALE

THE CROSS DISAPPEARED at thirty thousand feet.

I watched my grandmother's fingers work the clasp of her simple gold chain. She removed the small pendant—the cross she had worn every day of my remembered life— and slipped it into her purse. Then she put the chain back on, now empty of its symbol, and turned to look out the window as if nothing had happened.

I wanted to ask her why. The question sat on my tongue like a stone. But something in her movements, something deliberate and practiced, told me this wasn't the first time she'd done this. I swallowed my question and stared at the seat back in front of me.

Below us, somewhere in the darkness of the Indian Ocean, an island paradise was waiting. A grand wedding. Wealthy relatives. A world I had only seen in Bollywood films.

I had no idea that within days, I would face the same choice my grandmother had just made.

And I had no idea that my answer would be different.

. . .

THE FIRST COVER-UP

Two thousand years before that flight, another group of people faced a similar decision— and their choice echoes through history as a warning to everyone who follows.

The morning sun hadn't yet crested the Jerusalem hills when the soldiers stumbled into the city. Their sandals scraped against the cobblestones in uneven rhythm—not the disciplined march of Rome's finest, but the staggering shuffle of men whose world had just shattered. These weren't ordinary guards returning from an ordinary watch.

These were elite Roman soldiers—handpicked, battle-tested, the kind of warriors who had stared down charging cavalry without flinching, who had held formation while arrows darkened the sky above them.

But something had broken them.

Their faces were the color of ash. Their hands trained to grip sword and shield through hours of combat—trembled like leaves in a storm. One of them kept glancing over his shoulder, as if expecting the blinding light to find him again. Another moved his lips in silent prayer to gods who suddenly seemed very small.

They had felt the earthquake roll through the ground like a living thing. They had seen the angel descend—not floating gently like the spirits in their myths, but arriving with such terrible glory that their knees had buckled before their minds could even process what they were seeing.

They had watched the massive stone roll away from the tomb's mouth as if it weighed nothing, moved by an invisible hand that made Roman engineering look like a child's toy. The tomb was empty. And they knew exactly why.

What do you do when you've witnessed a resurrection? The Resurrection. The moment that split history in two.

If you're these soldiers, you run straight to the chief priests. Not to Pilate, their commanding officer—though that's where military protocol demanded they go.

Perhaps they sensed that what they'd witnessed belonged more to the realm of the sacred than the military. Perhaps they simply didn't know where else to turn with news that defied everything they understood about death and power and the finality of Roman execution.

The priests listened, their faces carefully composed even as their minds raced. And then they did what powerful people have always done when truth threatens their position.

They reached for their wallets.

PARADISE CALLING

Let me take you back to how I ended up on that plane, watching my grandmother tuck away the symbol of everything we believed.

My aunt—my father's sister—had married a successful

Muslim doctor she'd met in medical school. They lived on a gorgeous island nation in the Indian Ocean, the kind of place where Bollywood filmed all those romantic movies with pristine beaches and swaying palms, where the water was so clear you could count the fish swimming beneath your feet.

Every time she visited India, it was an event. She brought chocolates from places I'd only seen in movies, clothes that made us feel like royalty, and toys that became the envy of every kid on our street.

She would give us children money too—crisp bills that felt like treasure in our hands. Her visits meant celebration.

But after my father's disappearance in 1990, something shifted in how she looked at me. I carried traces of my father in my face, echoes of his expressions in my smile. She would sometimes pause mid-conversation just to study me, her eyes softening with memory and grief.

Among all her nieces and nephews, she held me closest, as if by loving me, she could somehow keep her brother near.

One summer, she arrived with her youngest daughter, who was about to be married. The wedding would take place on the island. And she wanted me there.

Me. A boy who had never left India. Someone whose world consisted of the streets of Lucknow and the stories I heard about places beyond.

She paid for my passport, bought my ticket, arranged my visa. When word spread among our relatives and friends that I was flying to this island paradise, I became something of a celebrity. Everyone wanted to know what it would be like. I couldn't tell them yet. I was too busy imagining.

The night of our departure from New Delhi, I could barely contain myself. We boarded the aircraft, and I'll admit —at that age, I was most excited about the plane food.

Twenty-five years and countless flights later, I barely glance at those aluminum-wrapped trays. But back then? It was part of the adventure.

That's when it happened. That's when I watched my grandmother remove her cross. And that's when something inside me—something I couldn't yet name—began to stir.

A BEAUTIFUL CAGE

The views before landing were breathtaking. Turquoise waters, white beaches, green mountains rising from the sea. It looked exactly like the movies, only more vivid, more alive.

When we landed and stepped onto the tarmac, I breathed air cleaner than anything I'd ever experienced. The roads were immaculate, the streets orderly, the colors somehow more saturated than anything I'd known in India.

My aunt's house was enormous—prepared for a wedding that would span multiple days, multiple functions, multiple celebrations. I met relatives I'd only heard of in passing, cousins whose faces I was seeing for the first time, extended family members who welcomed me warmly into their world.

For a few days, I floated in a dream. This was paradise.

Then my aunt pulled me aside.

"Abba," she said, her voice kind but firm, "you're going to meet many people here. When they ask your name, just tell them your nickname—Abba." and not Norman.

In India, everyone has a home name, a nickname used by family and close friends. Mine is Abba, named after the Swedish band because my father—whose nickname was

Baba - wanted our names to rhyme. It was nothing unusual for relatives to call me Abba.

But that wasn't why my aunt was asking. She further said something that hit me like a lightning bolt, ***"don't tell anyone that you are a Christian."***

She was asking because Norman Morris Gray is unmistakably Christian. In India, names carry identity like flags. The Patels are from Gujarat. The Singhs are from Punjab. The biblical names—the Davids, the Johns, the Normans—these belong to Christians.

My name announced my faith to anyone familiar with Indian culture.

My aunt didn't want her husband's family—her Muslim in-laws and relatives—to know that her brother's son was a Christian.

Before I could process this, she added something else."When we eat at the dining table, don't pray over your food. If you need to pray, do it in your room before you come down."

Three requests. Simple enough, perhaps. Easy enough to follow. After all, she had paid for everything. She had given me this incredible opportunity. What was a small compromise in exchange for such generosity?

But something inside me cracked.

Now I understood why my grandmother had removed her cross at thirty thousand feet. I want to be clear about something: my aunt is a genuinely good person. She has given generously to underprivileged relatives her entire life.

She showed me nothing but kindness even as she made these requests.

I don't know what pressures she faced from her in-laws, what compromises she'd learned to make over the years, what unspoken rules governed life in that household.

But I was young, and my faith was the most precious thing I had.

After my father vanished, after we lost everything, after people who once called us friends suddenly looked through us like we were ghosts—the church remained. Jesus remained.

My identity as a Christian wasn't just a label; it was the ground beneath my feet when everything else had turned to sand.

And now I was being asked to hide it.

THE COST OF SILENCE

Matthew tells us what happened next in Jerusalem. The chief priests called an emergency meeting with the elders. The tomb was empty. The guards were talking. Something had to be done.

Their solution was elegant in its simplicity: bribery.

Picture the scene. The guards stood in the chamber, still pale, still shaken. The priests counted out the coins—silver catching the lamplight, clinking against each other as they piled up. A small fortune, growing larger with each piece added to the pile. The guards watched the money accumulate, and slowly, you could see something shift in their eyes.

The terror of what they'd witnessed began to dim. The

blinding light of the angel became easier to doubt. The earthquake? Perhaps they'd imagined it. The stone rolling away? Surely there was another explanation.

"You are to say, 'His disciples came during the night and stole him away while we were asleep,'" the priests instructed. And to sweeten the deal: "If this report gets to the governor, we will satisfy him and keep you out of trouble."

Think about what they were asking. Roman soldiers falling asleep on watch was a capital offense. These guards were being asked to confess to dereliction of duty—a crime punishable by death—in exchange for money and a promise of protection.

They were being asked to trade the most astonishing truth in human history for a bag of coins and a political favor.

The silver was heavy in their hands. The priests' promise hung in the air. And the memory of what they'd actually witnessed—the light, the earthquake, the empty tomb, the angel— began to feel like a dream they could choose to forget.

Matthew tells us, with devastating simplicity: "So the soldiers took the money and did as they were instructed."

Eyewitnesses to the resurrection, bought and silenced.

SEND ME HOME

I found my grandmother and told her everything. I was shaking. The paradise outside the window suddenly felt like a prison. The beautiful house felt like a cage. I wanted to go home.

"Send me back to India," I pleaded. "I can't do this. I can't hide who I am."

She tried to calm me, but I was resolute. I told her that I know why she had removed her cross on the plane. She too had learned to hide, to compromise, to tuck her faith away when it became inconvenient.

I couldn't do it. The irony wasn't lost on me. Here I was, a poor kid from a family that had lost everything, standing in a mansion belonging to wealthy relatives, with every material comfort at my fingertips—and I was ready to walk away from all of it rather than deny my Lord.

But isn't that exactly the choice?

The soldiers had a price. The chief priests found it. The question life asks each of us is simple: What's yours?

What would it take for you to stay silent about what you know to be true? What amount of money, what level of comfort, what promise of protection would convince you to tell a different story than the one you've witnessed?

TAKING A STAND

I didn't leave the island. I stayed all forty-five days. But I stayed on my terms.

One evening, I found my cousin in the kitchen. She had shown me nothing but warmth since I'd arrived. I took a breath. "Shabnam, can you take me to church on Sunday?"

Her face lit up—not with surprise or discomfort, but with genuine delight. "Of course! I know exactly where there's a church."

I was expecting hesitation from her, but I was surprised how quickly she accepted my request.

That Sunday, she drove me to a small church nestled between palm trees. She parked outside and smiled. "I'll come back when it's over," she said. "Take your time."

A Muslim woman had driven her Christian cousin to worship Jesus—and in doing so, had encountered something that would stay with her long after I left the island.

Word spread through the house. The Christian nephew had gone to church. No one confronted me. No one rebuked me. But they knew where I stood. I wasn't for sale.

Something remarkable happened over the remaining weeks. The very identity I'd been asked to hide became a bridge rather than a barrier. Conversations grew deeper.

Relatives who had seen me as just another visiting nephew began to see me as someone with convictions, someone who stood for something. Respect—genuine respect —began to replace awkward avoidance.

I went to a different church every Sunday and met several pastors who would later become instrumental in what God had planned for my return.

THE RETURN

Five years later, I returned to that same island. But this time, everything was different. I had just planted a church in Chandigarh. I brought with me a friend—Sunny, who had co-planted the church with me. We weren't there for a wedding. We were there for a two-week preaching tour.

Sunny came from a Hindu background. He had grown

up performing *pujas*, celebrating Diwali, knowing nothing of Jesus beyond the fact that Christians existed somewhere in his country.

Then he encountered the risen Christ—not through argument or persuasion, but through an undeniable experience of God's presence that shattered everything he thought he knew.

He left behind not just his religion but his family's expectations, his community's approval, his entire framework for understanding the world. *He wasn't for sale either.*

The pastors I had met during my first visit—the ones I'd quietly connected with even while being told to hide my faith—they all wanted me to preach in their churches.

Different pastors came to my aunt's house nearly every day, picking us up for meetings and services across the island.

My aunt watched all of this with wonder. "How do you know all these people?" she asked. And I had the perfect opportunity to share about the greatest institution on earth—the Church.

The very faith I'd been asked to conceal had become the source of influence and connection that now opened doors across an entire nation.

The relatives who had once been kept at a careful distance from my Christianity were now intrigued. They wanted to know about Sunny—how had this Hindu man come to follow Jesus? We talked openly about faith. We watched Christian television in their living room. We prayed without hiding.

The cross that my grandmother had tucked away in her purse was now being proclaimed in conversations over chai.

• • •

THE TRUTH HAS RESURRECTION POWER

Here's what those Roman soldiers never understood: truth cannot be permanently buried. Lies require maintenance. Cover-ups demand constant vigilance. But truth? *Truth is patient. Truth waits. Truth has resurrection power.*

The story those guards were paid to tell—"His disciples stole the body"—became the official explanation. Matthew notes that "this story has been widely circulated among the Jews to this day." It worked, at least for a while, at least for some people.

But here's the thing about that lie: it required believing that a group of frightened disciples who had abandoned Jesus and fled, who were hiding behind locked doors in terror, somehow found the courage to overpower elite Roman guards, roll away a massive stone, and steal a body—all while those battle-hardened soldiers slept.

The lie was never really believable. It was just convenient.

And look at where we are now, two thousand years later. The story those soldiers were paid to suppress has spread to every continent.

The resurrection they witnessed and denied is celebrated by billions.

The name they were bribed to dishonor is the name above every name.

The cover-up failed. Truth won.

· · ·

WHAT'S YOUR PRICE?

What does it mean to be "not for sale"?

It means understanding that your integrity has no price tag. It means recognizing that the moment you accept payment for silence, you've lost something no amount of money can buy back.

Those soldiers traded their testimony for coins. The coins are long spent. The soldiers are long dead. But the resurrection they witnessed and denied continues to transform lives daily.

My grandmother traded her visible faith for family peace. I don't judge her—I don't know what pressures she faced, what calculations she made, what costs she weighed. But I know this: the cross she removed from her neck still belonged to her. She just chose not to let others see it.

I decided that day, as a young adult in paradise, that I would never remove my cross. Not from around my neck, and not from my life.

This isn't about being confrontational or obnoxious. I didn't march through my aunt's house demanding everyone acknowledge my Christianity. I didn't pick fights or make scenes. I simply refused to pretend I was something I wasn't.

There's a difference between wisdom and compromise.

Wisdom knows when to speak and when to be silent. Compromise knows the price of silence and agrees to pay it.

. . .

EVERYONE HAS A PRICE

Here's what I know after all these years of following Jesus: Everyone has a price in someone's mind. There will always be someone who thinks they can buy your silence, purchase your compromise, negotiate your convictions.

In seventeen years of pastoral ministry, I've watched people face their price.

I've seen a young man abandon his faith for a woman who told him to choose between her and Jesus. He chose her. The marriage lasted three years. His regret has lasted much longer.

I've watched a businessman water down his testimony, inch by inch, deal by deal, until the man who once led Bible studies couldn't remember the last time he'd mentioned God outside church walls. The contracts kept coming. The conviction kept fading.

I've counseled parents who raised their children in faith, then taught them to hide it at prestigious schools where Christianity might harm their prospects. They bought the silence with tuition checks, and now wonder why their adult children have no faith to hide.

The question isn't whether you'll face the offer. The question is whether you'll take it. The Roman guards took the money. The religious leaders wrote the check. And for a brief moment, it seemed like a successful transaction. The story was controlled. The narrative was managed. The resurrection was contained.

Except it wasn't.

. . .

Because you can't buy a resurrection. You can't bribe a stone to roll back. You can't pay an angel to keep quiet. You can't purchase enough silence to stop truth from rising.

The guards had witnessed the single most important event in human history. They had front-row seats to the moment that changed everything. The angel appeared. The earth shook. The Son of God walked out of His grave.

And they sold that testimony for money that wouldn't last and protection that couldn't save.

WHAT REMAINS

I know what it means to lose everything—security, status, respect, certainty. I learned what it felt like when people who smiled at you yesterday look through you today. But I also learned what remains when everything else is stripped away.

Jesus remains. The resurrection remains. The identity I have in Christ—that remains. No amount of money can buy it. No amount of pressure can crush it. No amount of compromise can improve it.

I am a child of the living God. I am a follower of the risen Christ. I am not ashamed of the gospel, because it is the power of God for salvation.

Whatever paradise someone is offering you, whatever comfort they're promising, whatever protection they're guaranteeing—if the price is your testimony, if the cost is your witness, if the deal requires you to hide your cross... Walk away.

Because the resurrection is worth more than anything they can offer. And the One who rose from the dead is worth everything you could ever give.

THE FINAL VERDICT

The soldiers took the money and told the lie. I stayed on the island and told the truth.

Two thousand years from now, which choice will have mattered?

You already know the answer.

My grandmother put her cross back on before we landed in India. I don't know if she ever took it off again. But I know this: I watched her remove it at thirty thousand feet, and I decided that day that I will not take off my cross—not for paradise, not for peace, not for any price anyone could name.

And I am not for sale. Neither are you.

NO MORE STORIES: Just Truth

I'm not going to repeat what you've already read. You've walked with me through the stories. You've seen the miracles and the mess, the faith and the failure. You know my family now. You know my scars.

So let me just talk to you.

Somewhere along the way, many of us learned to believe in the resurrection without being changed by it. We learned the right answers. We can defend the empty tomb in an argument. We know He rose. We'd bet our lives on it.

But we wouldn't change our lives for it.

And that's the gap I've been trying to close in these pages—the distance between what we say we believe and how we actually live. Because I've stood in that gap myself. I've preached resurrection on Sunday and lived like a practical atheist by Wednesday. I've sung about victory while nursing defeat in my heart.

I'm not pointing fingers. I'm confessing. And I'm inviting you into the same honesty.

. . .

Because here's what I've learned after decades of following Jesus, after planting churches, after nearly losing my wife, after holding a son the doctors said was dead: theology that doesn't transform you will eventually bore you. Beliefs that don't cost you anything will eventually mean nothing to you.

The resurrection isn't a doctrine to be defended. It's a reality to be inhabited.

WHAT I SEE

Let me tell you what I see when I look at the church today.

I see people who are exhausted from performing a faith they've never possessed. I see believers who have been in church their whole lives but have never let the earthquake touch them. I see pastors running on empty, leading people to a well they haven't drunk from themselves in years. I see young people walking away because they've never seen resurrection faith lived out—only resurrection faith talked about.

And I see myself in all of it. That's why this book exists.

I didn't write this to condemn the church. I wrote it because I love the church. I've given my life to her. I've bled for her. And it breaks my heart to watch people settle for a Christ they keep safely buried when a living Savior is available to them.

We have domesticated the most dangerous faith in human history. We have turned the Lion of Judah into a house cat. We have made Jesus safe, predictable, manageable —and in doing so, we've robbed ourselves of the very power that raised Him from the dead.

That power isn't reserved for Bible characters and missionaries. It's for you. Right now. Today. In your office, your kitchen, your hospital room, your broken marriage, your failing business, your secret addiction, your quiet despair. ***The same Spirit that walked Jesus out of that tomb lives in you.***

So why do we live like He's still dead?

THE INCONVENIENCE OF RESURRECTION

I think it's because resurrection is inconvenient.

A dead Jesus makes no demands. He fits neatly into our schedules. We can visit His grave on Sunday, leave our flowers of worship, and go back to running our own lives. A dead Jesus doesn't ask us to forgive the person who destroyed us. He doesn't tell us to sell our comfort and follow Him. He doesn't flip tables in the temples we've built to our own success.

But a living Jesus? He's uncontrollable. He shows up when you least expect Him. He asks for things you don't want to give. He sends you to places you don't want to go. He loves people you'd rather avoid. He insists on being Lord of everything or nothing.

And most of us, if we're honest, have negotiated Him down to a few rooms in our house. We gave Him the Sunday room. Maybe the crisis room—we'll call on Him when things fall apart. But the money room? The ambition room? The relationship room? The secret room we don't let anyone see?

Those doors stay locked.

And Jesus stands on the other side, the same Jesus who walked through locked doors after His resurrection, and He waits. He doesn't force entry. He knocks. He invites.

But make no mistake—He wants the whole house.

TO THOSE WHO ARE TIRED

I need to say something to those of you who are tired.

I know you're out there. I know because I've been you. Ministry has drained you. Life has battered you. You've given and given and given, and you feel like there's nothing left. The joy you once had has faded into duty. The fire has become routine. You're still showing up, but something inside you has gone quiet.

Can I tell you something? ***The resurrection isn't just for the lost. It's for the empty.***

Jesus didn't only come to save sinners. He came to raise the dead. And sometimes the deadest places aren't in those who've never known Him—they're in those of us who've known Him so long we've forgotten what it felt like to encounter Him.

You need resurrection too. Not just once, at conversion. Again. Today.

Come to the tomb. Look inside. Remember what it was like when you first believed, when the reality of the risen Christ hit you and nothing else mattered. That Christ hasn't changed. That power hasn't diminished. The problem isn't that He's become less alive— it's that we've become more numb.

So ask Him to wake you up. Ask Him to do it again. Because He will. He's in the business of bringing dead things back to life. That includes your passion. That includes your calling. That includes you.

TO THOSE WHO ARE AFRAID

And to those of you who are afraid—you've wandered too far, wasted too much, failed too completely—I need you to hear this.

The resurrection means it's never too late.

Do you understand what happened when Jesus walked out of that tomb? He didn't just conquer His own death. He conquered the finality of every death. Every failure. Every ending that felt permanent.

The grave couldn't hold Him. And whatever grave you think you're stuck in cannot hold you either—not if you call on the name of the One who got up and walked out.

I've watched people who had every reason to quit find new life in Jesus. I've watched marriages everyone gave up on get resurrected. I've watched prodigals come home. I've watched addicts set free. I've watched hope return to eyes that had gone dark.

That's resurrection. That's what happens when you stop living like Jesus is dead and start living like He's alive and actively working in your situation.

Your story isn't over. The tomb is empty. And that means your ending hasn't been written yet.

. . .

TO THOSE WHO HAVEN'T SURRENDERED

Now, let me speak to those of you who know the truth but haven't surrendered to it.

You've read this book. You've nodded along. You believe Jesus rose from the dead— intellectually, you're convinced. But nothing has changed. Your life tomorrow will look exactly like your life yesterday.

I say this with love, but I say it directly: belief without surrender is not faith. It's just agreement.

The demons believe Jesus rose from the dead. They were there. They saw it. They tremble at His name. But they haven't bowed. They haven't surrendered. They know who He is without letting Him be their Lord.

And I fear that too many of us are living the same way— convinced of resurrection but untransformed by it. We have the information without the implication. The theology without the trajectory.

Something has to shift. Not in your head—in your life.

What would it look like if you actually lived this week as though Jesus is alive? What decisions would you make? What conversations would you have? What would you stop hiding? What would you start doing?

That's not a rhetorical question. I want you to answer it. Right now. Before you close this book.

. . .

THE CHURCH I DREAM OF

The church I dream of isn't a church that has better arguments for the resurrection. It's a church that makes the resurrection undeniable by how we live.

When the world looks at us, they shouldn't just hear us talking about a risen Savior. They should see Him. In our love that doesn't make sense. In our forgiveness that defies logic.

In our generosity that seems reckless. In our joy that circumstances can't steal. In our peace that passes understanding. That's the apologetic no one can argue with. Not words about resurrection—lives that prove it.

I've been to churches where the theology was perfect and the people were dead. I've been to gatherings where they couldn't articulate a creed but the presence of God was so thick you could barely breathe. Give me the second one every time.

Because resurrection isn't an idea. It's a person. And He doesn't want to be studied. He wants to be encountered, followed, obeyed, loved.

THE CHARGE

So here's my charge to you. Not as someone who has arrived, but as someone walking the same road, fighting the same fight, chasing the same risen King.

Live like it's true.

When you wake up tomorrow, remember that the tomb

is empty and act accordingly. Pray like you're talking to someone who actually hears you—because you are. Worship like you're in the presence of the King of Kings—because you are. Give like your treasure is stored in an unshakable kingdom—because it is. Love the difficult people in your life like Jesus loved you when you were His enemy—because He did.

Stop tiptoeing around your faith like it's something to be embarrassed about. Stop hiding your cross. Stop shrinking back. Stop playing it safe.

You follow a Savior who invaded death's territory and walked out victorious. You carry the same Spirit that raised Him from the dead. You belong to a kingdom that cannot be shaken.

So why are you living like someone with no hope?

YOUR TOMB

I don't know what tomb you've been staring at. I don't know what stone feels too heavy to move. I don't know what situation you've declared dead and buried.

But I know this: the same power that raised Christ from the dead is available to you. Not in theory. Not in sentiment. In reality.

And the only question left isn't whether that's true. The evidence is in. History has rendered its verdict. The resurrection happened.

The only question left is whether you'll live like it did. Will you?

· · ·

THE EARTHQUAKE CONTINUES

The earthquake is still rumbling. The ground beneath your feet is shifting. Everything that can be shaken is being shaken so that what cannot be shaken will remain.

And in the middle of it all, heaven sits in perfect peace. Not anxious. Not scrambling. At rest. Because the work is finished. The victory is won. Death has been swallowed up.

All that remains is for you to step into it. To live from it. To stop standing at the tomb and start walking in resurrection.

Jesus is alive. Now go live like you believe it.

The world is watching. They've heard our songs. They've read our bumper stickers. They've seen our social media posts.

Now they're waiting to see if any of it is real. Show them.

THE DEAD JESUS?

NO.

THE LIVING JESUS.

AFTERWORD

What you have just read from Norman Gray is not merely a collection of testimonies or reflections. It is a spiritually provocative call to live in the reality of the resurrection. Chapter by chapter, through personal narrative and biblical exposition, the message is clear: there is a gap between believing in the resurrection and living in its power. The only question that ultimately matters is whether we will live as though Jesus is truly alive.

I have had the privilege of witnessing Norman's journey of faith firsthand. From him living in my home to laboring together in ministry across nations, I can say with deep joy, "This is my son, in whom I am well pleased." What his life — and now these pages — prove is that one can intellectually affirm the resurrection and yet remain practically unchanged. But you do not truly know Jesus unless you know the power of His resurrection.

Norman has lived what he proclaims. From planting churches across India to ministering across continents, he has preached Christ faithfully — not for platform or notoriety, but because the Jesus he loves is alive. He has spent time in homes, discipled believers, and given his life to declaring this singular message: Jesus lives.

When he cried out to the living God for his wife Supriya — the love of his life — it was the living God who comforted him, answered him, and performed miracles again and again. Resurrection power was not theory; it was experienced reality.

As he writes, many believers give Jesus limited access — Sunday faith, crisis faith — while keeping certain rooms locked: finances, ambition, hidden sin, relationships. But the risen Christ wants the whole house. This is where you must begin. Your situation is not hopeless.

Hope is not fragile when it is rooted in the resurrected Lord. That hope can be transferred generationally. Adriel and Andrew, the sons of this man of God, have grown up hearing Jesus prayed to in every room of their home. They have heard the songs, the testimonies, the preaching. In them you see what it looks like when Christ has unrestricted access to every room of a life.

The strongest apologetic for the resurrection is a resurrected people.

We follow a Savior who conquered death — so why live as though hope is fragile? Throughout this book, one central question echoes: The resurrection is historically credible, theologically defended, and doctrinally affirmed. The only remaining question is this:

Will you live like it happened?

This is not a book written merely for your inspiration. It was read by you — but it is not just for you. If you allow its message to ignite your life as it has ignited Norman's, you will witness dry bones rise around you as you declare dead things come alive in the Name of Jesus.

In His Grip,
Pastor Tyrone P. Jones
Lead Pastor, Church for the City
Yuma, AZ

Thanks to my wife, Supriya! You have been my strength in all the low and slow seasons since we got married. You have been a pillar of faith in our home. Your presence, encouragement, and constant support have made this book possible. Thank you for fearlessly walking with me in the seasons where I felt lost. You are my great joy. I love you.

Thanks to my sons, Adriel and Andrew! As a father, I am proud of you both. In this season, I have not been able to provide every need of yours, but thanks for understanding that this was just a season. The season changes now. Thanks for not demanding anything, knowing your father had very limited resources. I love you both and believe that you both will serve the Lord all the days of your lives.

Thanks to my mother, Veena! You gave me life and took us to church, where I received eternal life in our living Lord and Savior Jesus Christ. Your legacy will live on through generations.

Thanks to my sister, Jyoti, and brother, Marvin, for all the wonderful childhood memories. We had nothing but God. Look what the Lord has done in and through all of us. He gave us wonderful spouses and children who love and serve the Lord. I wish we could spend more time together. Thank you for the memories of a lifetime.

Thanks to my Pastor, Augustus Anthony! You have been a father to me. Through all these years you have been constant, and I have looked up to you. I love the Word of God because of you. You made the Church come alive for me. I am better because of you.

Thanks to the only man I call Dad in this world, Pastor Tyrone Pernell Jones! You welcomed me into your family and life as your own. It is because of you that I have order in my life. You made me fall in love with preaching the Word with clarity and conviction. My life has never been the same. Thanks for calling me your son.

Thanks to my home church, Assembly of Believers Church, Sujanpura, in Lucknow, India, for showing me that Jesus is alive and that all things are possible to those who believe in Him. You are the best church in the world.

Thanks to the only church I have pastored, Assembly of Believers Church, Chandigarh. You have my heart. A people I can call my own. A city and church that gave me everything I have today. A place that taught me the biggest lessons of my life. You are the best church I have ever pastored and still oversee.

Thanks to all the wonderful pastors, friends, co-workers, and ministry partners who took the time to review these chapters.

Your input and critique have shaped this book. You will always have a special place in my heart.

Thanks to my dear friend, Pastor Robin Steele, for making it possible for our family to move to America—the greatest country on the planet. You have gone above and beyond for us. Thank you for being so generous. You are a source of joy and encouragement. Our family is grateful, and we love you.

Thanks to my PromiseLand family. You have all received our family with open arms. Our family has been given so much love from you that we could never repay it. Thanks for all the friendships we have made here. You truly are a real representation of heaven — people from all walks of life and all colors coming together to worship one God.

Thanks to my Sonrise India Board members for believing in me and in the vision God has given me to plant churches. Through these years of knowing and serving alongside you, you have enabled me to be bold in my faith, prayerful in my efforts, and joyful in serving the Body of Christ.

Thanks to my pastor friends all over the world. It gives me so much joy to visit your homes and churches. Your friendship and presence in my life mean the world to me.

Thanks to all who have sown financially into this book project. You made it possible for the world to read this message of His resurrection. Keep sowing into His Kingdom.

Above all, thank You, Jesus—my Lord and Savior. My life would be worthless without You. You chose me from a small city in India and took me all over the world to preach the Gospel. I had no idea how my life would unfold when I gave You my heart. You have been my constant, my source, and my refuge. I will continue to live for You until my last breath.

USE ME LORD. HERE I AM.

ABOUT THE AUTHOR

Pastor Norman Morris Gray is, above all else, a husband and father. He lives in Texas with his wife, Supriya, and their sons, Eddie and Andy. For Pastor Norman, family is not separate from ministry—it is the foundation of it. Before he leads a congregation, he leads his household. He teaches, prays, models integrity, and guides his family in the ways of the Lord with quiet, daily faithfulness. To him, legacy is not built from platforms, it is built from a life well lived before God and those closest to you.

From that foundation, Pastor Norman serves as a visionary pastor, spiritual builder, and author whose life and ministry are marked by conviction and unwavering Kingdom alignment. His voice carries both pastoral compassion and prophetic clarity, calling people beyond passive church attendance into authentic, life-altering transformation.

Deeply rooted in devotion to Jesus Christ and yielded to the work of the Holy Spirit, his ministry centers on intimacy with God, spiritual maturity, and Spirit-led revival. His conviction is unwavering: the Church must be spiritually alive, doctrinally grounded, and courageous enough to confront the forces that quietly erode freedom. He believes order does not limit the Spirit but it makes room for Him.

A defining thread throughout his life is restoration and reconciliation. Pastor Norman carries firsthand understanding of seasons marked by silence, distance, and divine realignment. Rather than viewing those seasons as loss, he recognizes them as preparation. His testimony echoes a truth he preaches without apology: nothing surrendered to God is ever wasted.

As an author, Pastor Norman writes with urgency, pastoral depth, and fearless clarity. He does not write merely to inspire emotion — he writes to provoke alignment, awaken purpose, and call readers into obedience. The page, for him, is another pulpit. A church planter at heart, he has traveled to five continents, planting churches and preaching the Word of God with power in some of the most unreached corners of the world.

He is also a sought-after guest preacher, regularly ministering in churches across the globe, and remains open to every God-given opportunity to speak at churches and conferences wherever the Lord leads.

Pastor Norman Morris Gray continues to serve with a heart anchored in faith and eyes fixed on eternity. His message remains uncompromising:

One Kingdom. One Church. One direction — led by the Spirit of God.

And this is only the beginning. A new day is rising.

It's time for the SONRISE.

Follow Pastor Norman Morris Gray here-

@NORMANMORRISGRAY

instagram.com/normanmorrisgray

Sonrise India was established in 2018 under the leadership of Pastor Norman Morris Gray with a singular vision: to plant churches in the unchurched villages, towns, and cities of India.

Since its founding, the vision has expanded beyond India's borders to Nepal and Canada, where God is moving in a mighty way and souls are being saved, transformed, and added to His Kingdom.

Pastor Norman Morris Gray has been a faithful part of the Assembly of Believers Church in India, a movement that now encompasses over 1,100 churches across 24 states. Under the Spirit-led leadership of the founding Pastor, Augustus Anthony, thousands of leaders have been raised up and millions have come to the saving knowledge of our Lord and Savior Jesus Christ. Pastor Norman carries this legacy forward with boldness, planting churches in India and wherever God leads.

In recent years, Sonrise India Ministries has also stood alongside pastors and their families who have faced extreme persecution in India and Nepal—providing support, encouragement, and hope in the most difficult of seasons. We believe the Church does not retreat in the face of opposition, it advances.

We are continually seeking like-minded men and women who will partner with us in taking the Gospel to the most unreached places in India and around the world. There is much ground yet to be taken, and every hand matters. Together, we can spread the Gospel, care for orphans, and plant new churches in places that have never heard the name of Jesus.

Visit us at: **https://www.sonriseindia.org**

Please partner with us and give securely here-